Law and the Nation, 1865–1912

BORZOI BOOKS IN LAW AND AMERICAN SOCIETY

Law and the Nation, 1865–1912

Jonathan Lurie
Rutgers University
Newark

ALFRED A. KNOPF   NEW YORK

This book was originally developed as part of an American Bar Association program on law and humanities with major funding from the National Endowment for the Humanities and additional support from the Exxon Education Foundation and Pew Memorial Trust. The ABA established this program to help foster improved understanding among undergraduates of the role of law in society through the creation of a series of volumes in law and humanities. The ABA selected a special advisory committee of scholars, lawyers, and jurists (Commission on Undergraduate Education in Law and the Humanities) to identify appropriate topics and select writers. This book is a revised version of the volume first published by the ABA. However, the writer, and not the American Bar Association, individual members and committees of the Commission, the National Endowment for the Humanities, Exxon Education Foundation, or Pew Memorial Trust, bears sole responsibility for the content, analysis, and conclusion contained herein.

THIS IS A BORZOI BOOK
PUBLISHED BY ALFRED A. KNOPF, INC.

First Edition
9 8 7 6 5 4 3 2 1
Copyright © 1983 by Alfred A. Knopf, Inc.

LIBRARY OF CONGRESS CATALOGING IN PUBLICATION DATA

Lurie, Jonathan, 1939–
Law and the nation, 1865–1912.

(Borzoi books in law and American society)
Bibliography: p.
Includes index.
1. Law—United States—History and criticism.
I. Title. II. Series.

| KF366.L87 | 1982 | 349.73 | 82–14041 |
| | | 347.3 | |

ISBN 0-394-33195-8 (Paperbound)   394-33579-1 (Casebound)
Manufactured in the United States of America

Preface

These materials explore some developments of American legal history during the late nineteenth century; an era that, in the admittedly prejudiced view of this writer, remains one of the most fascinating of our entire past. Two major events were the focal points for developments discussed here. One was the conclusion and aftermath of the Civil War, the other was the rapid industrialization and corporate expansion that transformed American society. Unlike the 1930s and thereafter—when, in the wake of the New Deal and the depression, governmental planning assumed some importance—the years under consideration here were characterized by random responses to postwar problems and the course of industrialism. What policymakers intended to bring about is not as important historically as what actually took place. Similarly, what a people believe to have happened may be of great historical value in understanding what did in fact occur.

These generalizations are well illustrated by the four chapters that follow. It will be seen that the actual pieces of postwar legislation concerning both the ex-slave and business regulation may have been very different in results from intent. Moreover, what pro-Union Americans believed they were fighting about very strongly colored their attitudes toward federal authority in both economic regulation and civil rights. Also, C. C. Langdell may have intended only to "modernize" his law school's curriculum. But the context in which his reforms took place, along with other developments over which he had no control, contributed to a transformation of the legal profession by the turn of the century. Finally, by 1912 no one denied that rapid change had come to urban America. Yet how, to what extent, and with what speed the law should respond to the effects of industrialism were very difficult questions.

More than personal preference was involved in selecting these four topics. They are linked by several themes; First, they indicate the extent to which change was perceived as necessary for American society. In addition, they reveal the often concealed gap in the nation's legal history between intent and result. Equally important, I believe they illustrate a basic truth of the American legal system, which students should bear in mind—that frequently the law's solution to a problem will not be neat or efficient, nor even the result of a clear choice between two clearly defined alternatives. The ultimate solution may be neither black nor white, but rather reflect subtle shades of grey. It may not be a question of who is right or wrong, but rather who is "righter." Thus the ways in which a past generation saw the problems of its day, and the ways in which the current legal order confronts similar challenges of rights and regulations, may offer some insights into these contemporary issues, and some possibilities for their solution.

It should be noted, finally, that although some of the documents found herein may be familiar to the reader, the questions asked about them are probably different. They are designed to raise certain questions about law and the legal response to developments in the late nineteenth century. The materials assume some general familiarity with American political history from 1865 to 1912. They are intended, in other words, not to replace but to supplement readings in such courses as American history, American government, legal history, and business or economic history.

I wish to acknowledge the permission of Macmillan Publishers to quote from the Strong Diaries. I am also grateful to the Commission of the American Bar Association for the opportunity to prepare this volume; and to Jeffrey Longcope of Random House for his much appreciated assistance in bringing it to completion. For consistent encouragement and perceptive criticism, I remain very grateful to my friend and colleague Gerald Grob.

JONATHAN LURIE

Contents

Essay

Law and Individual Liberty: Some Contours of the Fourteenth Amendment

The Civil War did more than preserve the federal union, more than end American Negro slavery forever, more even than ensure the continued westward expansion of the United States. The war resulted in a potentially new relationship between the American citizen and the legal order. Over one hundred years after the war ended, that potentially new relationship is still evolving. There is no doubt, however, that in the late nineteenth century the potential was largely unfulfilled. Why was this the case?

Of the three accomplishments mentioned above, the generation that fought the Civil War regarded the first as the most important. As the war ran its course, and the issue of ending slavery assumed a greater place in public importance, still the belief in the sanctity of union, "the Union as it was," remained supreme. This union had been built on a firm base of federalism, which implied a national government of very limited functions, if not authority. Whereas today, the term "states' rights" carries with it justifiable implications of racism, such was not the case in the Civil War era. Advocacy of a strong union and devotion to states' rights were fully compatible attitudes. By 1861, several generations and an unbroken string of United States Supreme Court decisions had well established the idea that states' rights "stood for local control of the character of daily experience."[1]

Although an indigenous racism remained in the North, it was, rather, the *strong* support for federalism as it was known in the 1860s

---

[1] Phillip Paludan, *A Covenant with Death* (1975), p. 11.

that further blocked the United States from persistent and consistent efforts on behalf of the civil rights of ex-slaves. As Phillip Paludan has written, "the black man might be deprived of equal protection of the [state] laws not because he was hated, but because constitutionally established federalism was loved."[2] Since it had long been held that the Bill of Rights in the Constitution applied *only* to the federal government, remedies for alleged violations could come only from the states. Even at the state level, however, "Americans distrusted a governing power which they rarely encountered and almost never needed." The shape of American government, according to Thomas Carlyle, was "anarchy, plus a street constable."[3] Of course, Americans welcomed legal intervention when it would support economic enterprise, and "release energy." But again, especially in terms of individual, "law did not get in the way—it cleared the way."[4] Although many benefited from this attitude, blacks certainly did not.

As the Civil War dragged on, increasing in both intensity and suffering, the fact remained—whatever the publicly stated goals of the conflict had become—that the North fought primarily "a struggle for the familiar federal union."[5] Clearly, in peacetime few states were inclined to equalize civil rights of blacks with those of whites. "The federal government would have to transgress almost a century of history and break down the [established] division of power which allowed states but not Washington to determine the civil rights of citizens."[6] On the other hand, the war *had* become something by 1865 that it had not been in 1861. Whether the resulting momentum was enough to break the well-established mold of federalism became a central question. Rhetoric and reality confronted each other during Reconstruction. How enduring were past values? How great the determination to bring true equality to the ex-slave as well as to blacks in the Northern states?

The Thirteenth Amendment and the 1866 Civil Rights Act

According to Lincoln, the Civil War began as nothing more than an attempt to prevent an illegal act: secession. Even though the war lasted

---

[2] Ibid., pp. 12–13.
[3] Ibid., p. 15.
[4] Ibid., pp. 18–19.
[5] Ibid., p. 22.
[6] Ibid., p. 22.

four years, the federal government never admitted that secession had actually been accomplished. Hence its vigorous and ultimately successful drive to prevent any foreign recognition of the Confederacy. In this perception of the conflict, slavery appeared to play a distinctly unimportant role. Until 1863–1864, the key issue was survival of the Union, as Lincoln pointed out in 1862 in his answer to Horace Greeley, famed editor of the *New York Tribune,* who had demanded editorially that Lincoln free the slaves without delay. "My paramount object in this struggle," Lincoln wrote, "is to save the Union, and is not either to save or to destroy slavery. If I could save the union without freeing any slave, I would do it."[7]

Several years of war affected Lincoln's rather simplistic outlook. In 1864, with his Emancipation Proclamation already published, he wrote: "I claim not to have controlled events, but confess plainly that events have controlled me. Now, at the end of three years' struggle, the nation's condition is not what either party, or any man, devised or expected."[8] Even as Lincoln penned these words, Union forces were moving inexorably toward final victory. Indeed, die-hard Southern optimists notwithstanding, one can argue that there could not have been any real doubt of ultimate Southern defeat, given the vast resources of manpower, industrial strength, and agricultural resources available to the North.

An indication that Lincoln had gone far beyond his previous explanation for the outbreak of the war came in February 1865 with his strong support for the Thirteenth Amendment, which eliminated slavery as the United States had known it and empowered Congress to enforce this prohibition by "appropriate legislation" (see Documents, p. 79). The conflict, not *because* of Lincoln but rather *in spite* of him, had become one for freedom to the slave as well as a Union restored. There is no doubt that the framers intended to abolish slavery. However, since it had already been virtually ended by December 1865, when the new amendment was declared ratified, why did its authors add an enforcement clause? Some historians have argued that the amendment was intended not only as protection from "involuntary servitude and violence" but also to safeguard "all the full and equal rights of freedom, some of which history had identified and a multitude of which remained for the inscrutable future to reveal."[9] Why add an enforcement clause if

---

[7] *Collected Works of Abraham Lincoln,* ed. Roy Basler (1953), vol. 5, p. 338.
[8] Ibid., vol. 7, p. 282.
[9] Harold M. Hyman and William Wiecek, *Equal Justice Under Law* (1982), p. 390.

not to make it clear that Congress could now intervene to ensure that the fruits of four years of tragedy were not lost?

There is some justification for this view. It required no sophisticated understanding of constitutional principles that once slaves became free persons, they automatically acquired certain "civil rights." Indeed, it was the possession of these rights that set free men apart from slaves. The term "civil rights" had a definite meaning to the Civil War generation. Although it may well have meant to many what it means to us today, to a majority, civil rights probably meant economic rights— such as the right to own and sell property, to sue and be sued. The term, at least as far as many white Americans were concerned, did not refer to political or social rights.

Whether the framers of the Thirteenth Amendment actually intended the enforcement clause to implement an "open-ended national commitment about rights" remains, to this writer at least, uncertain.[10] There is no doubt, however, that *some* congressional figures did indeed so conclude. Thus the Ohio senator John Sherman claimed late in 1865 that the enforcement clause "gave Congress the express power 'to secure all...[Americans']' rights of freedom by appropriate legislation."[11] What was "appropriate" turned on how one responded to the rapidly moving political currents in 1865–1866, currents reflecting a variety of motives—reconciliation, revenge, restoration, reconstruction, racism, and Republicanism.

The 1866 act "to protect all persons in the United States in their Civil Rights, and furnish the Means of their Vindication" reflected growing Northern Republican fear that although defeated in war, the Confederacy might be victorious in peace. In the year after Lee's surrender, it became clear that while the reconstruction of Southern state governments was one thing, and fairly easily accomplished, the reconstruction of Southern society was quite another. With strength centered in the Northeastern and Midwestern sections of the country, the Republicans were in fact a Northern party trying to become national. With the party virtually unanimous in its determination that slavery had to be abolished but ill equipped to deal effectively with civil rights, unity foundered on the issue of what to do next.

The North had long been simultaneously antislavery and anti-Negro, with little awareness of the inherent inconsistency. Radical

[10] Ibid., p. 394.
[11] Ibid., p. 400.

Republicans such as Charles Sumner, the senator from Massachusetts, split the party through their efforts on behalf of black rights. For many Republicans as well as for Union Democrats the war had begun to save the Union. Then it had been expanded in scope to include emancipation. Now "misguided zealots" such as Sumner, who came from a state with a very small percentage of blacks, were insisting that the war aims include equality as well. With the war not yet over, a congressman from Lincoln's own state emphasized that "God has made the negro inferior, and ... laws cannot make him equal." Why should Sumner not go all the way, noted an observer, and "petition the Congress to change the negroes into white people?"[12]

More important even than this deep streak of Northern prejudice was a strong concern about the changing relationship between the states and the federal government. The basic tenet of federalism since the adoption of the Constitution had been that of a limited federal government, with control of local matters resting almost entirely with the states. Would any federal efforts undertaken on behalf of the ex-slave jeopardize this long-standing pattern? Were the ex-slaves entitled to any special treatment or protection? Did they not now stand before state law as free men like all others? Conceding that the blacks might indeed need special attention, especially in the Southern states, was such attention the responsibility of those states or of the federal government? Had the ex-slaves by virtue of their freedom now become American citizens? What, indeed, was an American citizen? What Lincoln's attorney general had written in 1862 remained valid in 1865: "I have often been pained by the fruitless search in our law books and the records of our courts for a clear and satisfactory definition of the phrase citizen of the United States."[13]

By early 1866, congressional Republican leaders had concluded, first, that President Andrew Johnson had been won over to the side of the old Southern-Whig-Conservatives, thus rendering him useless in furthering Reconstruction measures; and second, that the mere abolition of slavery plus legislation alleviating some of the physial wants of the blacks (the Freedmen's Bureau) was insufficient. With the Thirteenth Amendment as legal justification, there now had to be an additional statute protecting and guaranteeing basic civil rights—assuming some sort of consensus could be reached as to what those

---

[12] David Donald, *Charles Sumner and the Rights of Man* (1970), p. 157.
[13] Hyman and Wiecek, *Equal Justice*, p. 412.

rights were. As originally proposed to the Senate by Lyman Trumbull of Illinois, the first section of the Civil Rights Act of 1866 stated: "that all persons of African descent born in the United States are hereby declared to be citizens of the United States, and that there shall be no discrimination in civil rights or immunities among the inhabitants of any State or Territory of the United States on account of race, color, or previous condition of slavery."

Laws are first and foremost words, and thus the impact of a statute depends largely on what the words mean. What did Trumbull mean by "civil rights"? He replied: "The right to acquire property, and [the] right to go and come at pleasure, the right to enforce rights in the courts, to make contracts, and to inherit and dispose of property . . . and to full and equal benefit to all laws and proceedings for the security of person and property. These I understand to be civil rights, fundamental rights belonging to every man as a free man. . . . " Did the bill deal with "political rights"? Responded Senator Trumbull: "This bill has nothing to do with the political rights or status of parties. It is confined exclusively to their civil rights, such rights as should appertain to every free man."[14]

Although there was sharp criticism of this section, one senator denouncing the bill as "one of the most dangerous that was ever introduced into the Senate," the Senate approved the measure by a vote of 33 to 12. On March 1, 1866, the bill arrived at the House. Without waiting to be asked, Congressman James Wilson (sponsor of the bill in the lower chamber) focused on what "civil rights and immunities" meant. "Do they mean that in all things civil, social, political, all citizens without distinction of race or color, shall be equal? By no means can they be so construed. Do they mean that all citizens shall vote in the several states? No. . . . Nor do they mean that all citizens shall sit on the juries, or that their children shall attend the same schools. These are not civil rights or immunities." Civil rights, according to Wilson, meant "simply the absolute rights of individuals, such as the right of personal security, the right of personal liberty, and the right to acquire and enjoy property."[15]

In spite of Wilson's insistence on the limited scope of the 1866 bill, many Republicans objected to the civil rights section. Although Wilson agreed to add an amendment ("that nothing in this act shall be so construed as to affect the laws of any State concerning the right of

[14] *Globe,* 39 Cong., Part I, 1st Sess., 475–476.
[15] Alexander M. Bickel, "The Original Understanding," *Harvard Law Review,* 69 (1955), 16–17.

suffrage"), thus ensuring that the states could continue to control the right to vote, their doubts remained. John Bingham, a Republican representative from Ohio and the principal author of the as yet unwritten Fourteenth Amendment, criticized the first section of the proposed law on constitutional grounds. He noted, correctly, that numerous state constitutions in effect outside the South permitted some sort of racial discrimination. Passage of this federal statute, he argued, would put state judges in the impossible position of violating their state constitutions while enforcing the new law. Bingham implied that what was needed was not so much a federal statute as an amendment to the federal constitution, for there could be no doubt that such a provision would supersede any state statutes or constitutional clauses. The Ohio Republican urged the House to send the 1866 bill back to the Judiciary Committee with instructions to delete the civil rights section. Although the House refused to send it back with specific instructions, it did vote, by 82 to 70, to recommit the bill. Bowing to what may have seemed the inevitable, Wilson brought the civil rights measure back four days later without any reference to civil rights!

As amended, the bill easily passed the House, and the Senate concurred with the change. President Johnson vetoed the bill, claiming that while it purported to prevent discrimination against blacks, in reality it favored ex-slaves at the expense of the white race. Further, he insisted that the bill interfered with "the relations existing exclusively between a State and its citizens, or between inhabitants of the same State—an absorption and assumption of power by the General Government which, if acquiesced in, must sap and destroy our federative system of limited powers...." Indeed, the measure was not a step merely but a "stride" toward "centralization and the concentration of all legislative power in the national Government." Johnson also echoed Bingham's earlier point, holding that the bill "invaded the judicial power of the state."[16]

Nevertheless, both houses overrode Johnson's veto, and the Civil Rights Act of 1866 became law. It has apparently never been challenged successfully in a federal court, and thus it remains to this day the law of the land. Yet the points raised by Johnson troubled Republicans determined to protect the rights of the ex-slave while at the same time accepting the implacable racial realities of the country as a whole. (For the final text of the key section of the 1866 Civil Rights Act, see Documents, pp. 79–81.)

[16] *Globe*, 1858–1859.

The Fourteenth Amendment

Even as Congress awaited Johnson's reaction to the 1866 Civil Rights Act, the Committee of Fifteen—the congressional body charged with preparing reconstruction legislation—had begun consideration of an omnibus amendment that it was hoped would resolve several problems all at once. The Republicans (radicals and moderates alike) were concerned about the rapidity with which Johnson had welcomed ex-Confederate leaders back into important political positions in the former Confederate states. Further, they were fully aware that a Southerner (albeit one with Unionist principles) in the White House might well be able to appoint Southern-oriented justices to federal courts, including the United States Supreme Court. Moreover, with the midterm congressional elections coming up in the fall of 1866, radicals feared that returning Southern Democrats could also join with their Northern brethren to prevent the Congress from continuing its reconstruction measures or to revoke what had already been accomplished. Finally, the Republicans were equally clear that many in their own party, to say nothing of the "unreconstructed" South, were unprepared to see the blacks given more than what was absolutely necessary to ensure their equality before state law; and there was little agreement on what constituted that equality. A constitutional amendment could not be vetoed by the President or declared unconstitutional by a hostile Supreme Court. Moreover, it would be binding on all sections of the country, and thus it would indicate the Republicans' determination to make some sort of protection for the new black citizens an integral part of national policy.

In January 1866, the committee considering the proposed amendment received a suggested revision of the section dealing with political rights. As drafted by John Bingham, the section would have authorized Congress to make "all laws which shall be necessary and proper to secure all persons in every state full protection in the enjoyment of life, liberty and property; and to all citizens of the United States in any State the same immunities and also equal political rights and privileges." But the committee refused to approve this section. On February 3, Bingham produced a substitute that would enable Congress "to secure to the citizens of each State all privileges and immunities of citizens of the several States; and to all persons in the several States equal protection in the rights of life, liberty and property."[17] By a one-man vote margin, 7 to

---

[17] Bickel, "Original Understanding," p. 32.

6, the committee agreed to Bingham's proposal. Neither version made any reference to civil rights, and the later one deleted the earlier mention of political rights. Nevertheless, the proposal failed to pass the House. Critics objected less to the rights it gave blacks than to the vast powers it supposedly afforded the central government—another indication of the nineteenth-century respect for traditional federalism.

Not until April 1866 did the committee return to the subject of the proposed constitutional amendment. On April 21 a prominent Republican radical from Pennsylvania, Thaddeus Stevens, introduced another draft, which had been submitted to him by Robert Dale Owen, a well-known reformer. Section 1 of this proposal stated that "no discrimination shall be made by any state, nor by the United States, as to civil rights of persons because of race, color, or previous condition of servitude."[18] Section 2 provided that after July 4, 1876, exactly 100 years after the Declaration of Independence, "no discrimination shall be made by any state, nor by the United States as to the enjoyment...of the right of suffrage." Like the Massachusetts senator Charles Sumner, Stevens was in favor of immediate enfranchisement, whereas Owen argued that education was what the ex-slaves required. However, Stevens well knew congressional politics. What was principled might not be practical. Indeed, in 1866 it was not even possible. Thus Stevens reluctantly agreed with Owen that prospective suffrage might have a chance. In ten years perhaps the country as whole would be ready.

When the committee began consideration of the Owen-Stevens draft, Bingham proposed another section, that "no state shall make or enforce any law which shall abridge the privileges or immunities of citizens of the United States; nor shall any state deprive any person of life, liberty or property without due process of law; nor deny to any person within its jurisdiction the equal protection of the laws." The committee accepted the proposal 10 to 2. However, on April 25, for reasons that remain unclear, the members reversed themselves and by a 7-to-5 vote deleted Bingham's section from the amendment entirely. Three days later, the committee voted to make two additional changes.

The committee backed away from the original intention to grant suffrage prospectively and instead substituted a new section that removed "from the basis of representation persons to whom the vote was denied."[19] In other words, if 20,000 blacks were denied the right to vote, presumably the total figure on which the number of representatives were apportioned would be reduced by 20,000. The second change

[18] Ibid., p. 41.
[19] Ibid., p. 43.

involved the sudden revival of Bingham's section that had been deleted three days before. Now the persistent Ohio representative moved to substitute his section for the original civil rights section, and the committee—even though Bingham's wording made no reference to either political or civil rights—accepted his proposal by a vote of 10 to 3. Clearly, the Republicans were troubled about going forth to seek reelection with anything hinting at black suffrage, whether immediate or prospective.[20]

The House adopted the committee version of the amendment by a lopsided margin, 128 to 37, although the earlier vote to prevent amendments to it carried by only a 5-vote margin, 84 to 79. For its part, the Senate added a definition of American citizenship to the first section and backed away from another provision, endorsed by the House, that disenfranchised certain Southern voters until 1870. The House spent barely fifteen minutes on the Senate changes, approving them 120 to 32, and the Fourteenth Amendment went to the states for ratification in June 1866. It remains to this day what it probably was in that year, a group of sections, clauses, and words that meant and mean different things to different people. Few would deny, however, that it has become the most important amendment ever added to the American Constitution (see Documents, p. 81–82).

What did the framers intend in the Fourteenth Amendment? A seemingly endless amount of time and effort, as well as occasional very thorough scholarship, has been expended seeking answers to this question. Did they intend to bar discrimination? What about public discrimination as opposed to private acts? Did they intend to eliminate school segregation? Did they intend to make the Bill of Rights applicable to the states?

Detailed discussion of these questions is beyond the scope of this essay. Yet some important points should be made. The framers had no doubts that they were dealing not with a statute but with a change in a fundamental document of government—a constitution. They further knew that words can well change in meaning over time, just as constitutional meanings change over time—as indeed they had in the lifetimes of many of the amendment's framers. The commerce clause, for example, was not the same under Taney's Court as it had been under Marshall's. Moreover, they deliberately used very broad language in the

[20] Ibid., p. 44.

key parts of the amendment. It clearly was intended to apply to *all* parts of the country, including the South and the newly freed blacks.

Of this much there can be no doubt. Beyond this, however, the evidence is lacking. Is it not useless, therefore, to raise such a question as "Was the amendment intended to incorporate the Bill of Rights?" These questions merely attempt to make the past answer our problems, when the past may never have confronted them, thus leaving us no answer.[21] Moreover, convincing evidence on either side of the question has not been located. The framers said little on the subject, either in congressional debates or in the states. Even if their intentions were clear, however, they are not what matters historically. The crucial issue is the use to which the amendment was subsequently put. To paraphrase Justice Holmes, we should not worry so much about what the framers of the amendment meant. We should focus rather on what the amendment means.

Implict in this view of the matter is acceptance of the fact that the only permanent aspect of constitutional interpretation is change itself. Of course, the relationship between change and constitutional interpretation is not self-executing. It must be put into effect by the one agency that has the final say on what the constitution means. Whether the "law" that the United States Supreme Court is interpreting at any given time initiates change or responds to it, what matters in the end is less what the framers intended than what the justices conclude the amendment orders.

The importance of the Fourteenth Amendment for our time is well known. Since 1920 it has been the basis for applying several Bill of Rights amendments to the states, such as the First, the Fourth, the Fifth, and the Sixth. Regardless of what the framers intended, the Court has followed a practice of selective incorporation. In the period under consideration here, the late nineteenth century, almost 600 cases relying on the Fourteenth Amendment came to the Court. Less then 30 involved ex-slaves, and blacks appear to have won in only half a dozen instances.[22] If ex-slaves were not using the new amendment framed to protect their new freedom, who did make use of it, and how successful were they?

---

[21] William Nelson, "Legal and Constitutional History," *Annual Survey of American Law* (1976), 433.
[22] Forrest G. Wood, *The Era of Reconstruction* (1975), p. 37.

The Slaughter-House Cases and the 1875 Civil Rights Act

The first detailed discussion by the Supreme Court of the Fourteenth Amendment came in 1873 as the justices considered a case arising from a statute passed by the Louisiana legislature. The law gave one major slaughtering house in New Orleans the right to slaughter all beef, hogs, and other livestock, and forbade other butchers to do so in their own shops. The slaughtering was to be confined to the one area, and although other butchers could slaughter their own beef, they had to bring it to this central location first. A number of butchers who were not part of the favored group given the monopoly brought suit, claiming that they had received a *bum steer* (!). They based this contention largely on the recently enacted Fourteenth Amendment.

Mention has already been made of the quest for stability that marked the effort of post–Civil War America to cope with changes wrought by four years of conflict. As is readily seen, all parties, including the Court, agreed that the crucial question was what changes the new amendment required concerning the relationships between the states and their citizens (see Documents, pp. 87–107). The Supreme Court split 5 to 4, sustaining the Louisiana statute by the narrowest margin possible as a valid exercise of the police power. The majority, speaking through Justice Miller, a former doctor appointed to the Court by President Lincoln, concluded that the Fourteenth Amendment could not have been intended to change the well-established relationship between the states and their citizens, *with the exception of* the newly freed slaves. The latter enjoyed a special relationship to the federal government, one the states were now compelled to respect. We can only wonder what the outcome of this case would have been, had some of the plaintiffs been either black or ex-slaves. According to Miller, the plaintiffs seemed to have no standing to use the Fourteenth Amendment because it had not been written with them in mind. Thus by insisting that for the most part civil liberties and their vindication at law remained, as they always had been, the province of the states, the majority was able to avoid resolving the exact meaning of the due process and equal protection provisions of the new amendment.

The implication of the *Slaughter-house Cases,* namely that the new amendment protected only *federal* rights and immunities, leaving the rest to the states, troubled those who had viewed the enactment as providing protection to the former slaves from improper state and even private action. One solution might be to procure passage of another federal statute that would specify the rights to be protected. Charles Sumner, for example, had been trying since 1867 to have public school segregation declared illegal. He had met with no success, however, nor would such a measure be passed during his lifetime. A large number of Republicans were unwilling to support legislation that named specific civil rights, including public school integration. But these same congressmen were equally unwilling to go on record as favoring segregation.[23] From 1872 until his death two years later, Sumner used every opportunity he could grasp to force the Senate to consider, if not to adopt, a general ban on public discrimination. Typical of his efforts was a proposed statute he discussed on January 15, 1872, which would have entitled all citizens of the United States "without distinction of race, color, or previous condition of servitude" to the equal and impartial enjoyment of any accommodation, facility, or privilege furnished by common carriers, innkeepers, theaters, or other places of public amusement as well as by officials and teachers of common schools and other public institutions of learning. Fines, imprisonment, and court costs were to be levied against all persons convicted of violating the statute.

Sumner insisted that the emphasis on separate facilities was merely an artificial substitute for equality, a "contrivance by which a transcendent right, involving a transcendent duty is evaded."

> How vain [he said], to argue that there is no denial of Equal Rights when this separation is enforced. The substitute is invariably an inferior article. Does any Senator deny it? Therefore, it is not Equality. At best it is an equivalent only; but no equivalent is equality. Separation implies one thing for a white person and another thing for a colored person; but equality is where all have the same alike. There can be no substitute for equality; nothing but itself. Even if accommodations are the same, as notoriously they are not, there is no Equality. In the process of substitution the vital elixir exhales and escapes. It is lost and cannot be recovered; for Equality is found only in Equality.[24]

Although Sumner's words have for today's readers a disturbing ring of familiarity, they were largely ignored by his colleagues. Several

[23] Alfred H. Kelly, "The Congressional Controversy over School Segregation, 1867–1875," *American Historical Review*, 64 (1959), 544–545.
[24] *Globe*, 42 Cong., Part 1, 2nd Sess., 382–383. See also Donald, *Sumner*, pp. 531–539.

factors help to explain this condition. Mention has already been made of the ambivalence with which many Republicans and most Democrats regarded integration. Further, by 1872 the Republican party had split over the issue of a second term for President Grant—about whom the historian Henry Adams would later write that the process of evolution from Washington to Grant would have been enough to upset even Darwin. With one wing of the party, including Sumner, supporting a third-party candidate in the presidential election, the important issues seemed more concerned with budgets and corruption than with blacks and civil rights. Soundly defeated, Sumner's wing had even less influence within the party after 1872 than the little it had enjoyed before. Finally, the midterm congressional elections of 1874 resulted in a major victory for the Democrats in the lower house, where they would control the chamber for the first time since before the Civil War. Nevertheless, the fact that Sumner had died in March 1874, as well as the awareness that 1874–1875 represented the end of a major phase, if not *the* major phase of Reconstruction, led to passage early in February 1875 of the Civil Rights Act. Invoking Sumner's memory, while at the same time recognizing that the public mood seemed clearly against civil rights legislation, the final version was a far cry from the 1872 draft.

The statute started with a flowery preamble that noted "the equality of all men before the law" as well as the duty of government "to mete out equal and exact justice to all, of whatever nativity, race, color, or persuasion." It went on to declare "all persons within the jurisdiction of the United States" entitled to "full and equal enjoyment" of facilities and privileges concerning other places of public amusement. The new law made no mention of public schools at all.

Unlike the Civil Rights Act of 1866, the 1875 enactment received extended public comment, much of it critical. Less than two weeks after President Grant had approved the bill, the *Albany Law Journal* predicted that the Supreme Court would interpret the law as dealing "with the rights and privileges of the citizen as such, and not of citizens of the United States, and therefore, not within the legislative scope of Congress."[25] A lead article published in the July 1875 issue of the *Southern Law Review* commented: "That such a law can be practically enforced no intelligent person of either race or color believes." The article argued that the statute was patently unconstitutional and went on to quote a federal judge who had instructed a grand jury to that effect.

[25] *Albany Law Journal,* 11 (1875), 165–166.

What the new law forbade, such as exclusion from a hotel or theater on the grounds of race, was not an action that "Congress has any right to punish."[26] Here the writer was echoing the *Albany Law Journal* editorial. Finally, it is clear that during final debate on the proposed law, numerous congressmen had claimed the bill was unconstitutional.

The Civil Rights Cases (1883) and Plessy v. Ferguson (1896)

One of the fascinating characteristics of the American federal system is the way in which the Supreme Court decides when it is or is not appropriate to take up and resolve a particular case. It is as if the Court somehow has invisible antennae that it can figuratively extend, to sense better the prevailing national sentiment. Of course, on occasion—as in the Dred Scott case in 1857 and in a series of cases in the 1930s—the Court has misjudged the popular mood and retreated. But for the most part its antennae seem quite accurate. Perhaps a slightly cruder way of making the point is to note that "the Court follows the election returns." In any event, when it came to interpeting the 1875 statute, there was little wrong with the Court's perception of the prevailing public sentiment.

The genuine moral reform impulse that had played an important role in Reconstruction during 1865 had dissipated by 1875. Also important were a desire for national reconciliation and growing Northern awareness that Southern attitudes toward blacks were not very different from those of the rest of the country. Although it took place almost two years after the bill became a law, the famous "Compromise of 1876" ensured redeemer control of the South and did not intend active involvement by the federal government in protecting the civil rights of black Americans. The "law" predictably responded to these factors in 1883, when the Supreme Court declared the 1875 Civil Rights statute unconstitutional by a vote of 8 to 1 (see Documents, pp. 107–114). As for the ex-slave, supposedly under the protection of the federal law and constitutional amendments, Justice Bradley concluded:

> When a man has emerged from slavery, and by the aid of beneficent legislation has shaken off the inseparable concomitants of that state, there

[26] William A. Cocke, "Constitutionality of the Civil Rights Law," *Southern Law Review*, I [N.S.] (1875), 193–209.

must be some stage in the progress of his elevation when he takes the rank of a mere citizen, and ceases to be the special favorite of the laws, and when his rights as a citizen, or a man, are to be protected in the ordinary modes by which other men's rights are protected.

Speaking alone in dissent, Justice Harlan offered a very different analysis—both of the majority opinion and of the "true" intentions concerning the Fourteenth Amendment (see Documents, pp. 110–113).

The Civil Rights Act of 1875 had had virtually no effect on existing discrimination. The *Chicago Tribune* had called the measure harmless and unnecessary, while the *Nation* had described it as "amusing" and "tea-table nonsense."[27] Now, in 1883, the *Nation* observed that the "calm" with which the country accepted the Court decision revealed "how completely the extravagant expectations... of the war have died out." Nine-tenths of those who voted for the measure "knew very well," according to the writer, "that whenever it came before the Supreme Court it would be torn to pieces."[28] Actually, the law seems never to have been effectively enforced at all, even between 1875 and 1883.[29] Both the statute as worded and the decision of the Court eight years later show well that law is frequently an accurate reflection of the society from which it comes.

Little had changed by 1896 except that the tendencies already noted were even more prominent. In that year, the Supreme Court decided the question of whether the Fourteenth Amendment barred separate but supposedly equal public facilities—in this case, railroad cars. The decision in *Plessy v. Ferguson* had been foreshadowed both by the *Civil Rights Cases* and by Sumner's arguments more than twenty years before. By the mid-1890s not only was discrimination much more in evidence, especially in the South, but there now existed a substantial body of state case law, drawn from the North and the South, that supported this doctrine. In upholding the Louisiana statute that required separate railroad cars, Justice Brown endorsed the subtle but spurious connection between separate but equal that Sumner had rejected so decisively (see Documents, p. 114).

The Court split 7 to 1 on the *Plessy* case, with one justice not participating. Again Justice Harlan dissented, and again he saw beyond the immediate issues to a fundamental question concerning the direction

[27] James M. McPherson, "Abolitionists and the Civil Rights Act of 1875," *Journal of American History*, 52 (1965), 509.
[28] *Nation*, 36 (October 18, 1883), 326.
[29] McPherson, "Abolitionists," 509–510.

that American society ought to take. He insisted that this direction was made mandatory by the Fourteenth Amendment. The Court's action "puts the brand of servitude and degradation upon a large class of our fellow citizens, our equals before the law. The thin disguise of 'equal' accommodations for passengers in railroad coaches will not mislead anyone, or atone for the wrong this day done." As for the numerous state case precedents affirming separate facilities:

> Some, and the most important, of them are wholly inapplicable, because rendered prior to the adoption of the last amendments of the Constitution, when colored people had very few rights which the dominant race felt obliged to respect. Others were made at a time when public opinion, in many localities, was dominated by the institution of slavery; when it would not have been safe to do justice to the black man; and when, so far as the rights of blacks were concerned, race prejudice was, practically, the supreme law of the land. Those decisions cannot be guides in the era introduced by the recent amendments of the supreme law, which established universal civil freedom, gave citizenship to all born or naturalized in the United States and residing here, obliterated the race line from our systems of governments, national and state, and placed our free institutions upon the broad and sure foundation of the equality of all men before the law.[30]

Yet taken together with the rest of his dissent, there was some ambiguity in Harlan's opinion, which should be noted (see Documents, pp. 115–118).

With *Plessy,* the power of the Fourteenth Amendment to protect the civil rights of minority Americans reached its lowest point. Whatever the intentions of its framers may have been, the amendment apparently sanctioned separate but equal facilities. Further it appeared to apply only to state action. State inaction and private discrimination seemed not to be affected.

Again, it should be emphasized that this view had already been endorsed indirectly by the Supreme Court twenty years before *Plessy* was decided. The Fourteenth Amendment, as Justice Bradley had written in 1874, was "a guaranty of protection against the acts of the State government itself... not a guaranty against the commission of individual offenses." Chief Justice Waite, in his opinion for the Court dealing with the same case, had gone even further. The due process clause "does not add anything to the rights of one citizen as against another. . . . The duty of protecting all its citizens in the enjoyment of an

[30] *Plessy v. Ferguson,* 163 U.S. 537, 563 (1896).

equality of rights was originally assumed by the States, and it remains there." The federal government was, however, now obliged "to see that the States do not deny the right. This the amendment guarantees, and no more."[31] Homer Plessy, after reading the very few cases dealing with the rights of the ex-slave during the years 1873 to 1896, might well have doubted whether the Fourteenth Amendment had been of any lasting value to black America at all. Judges could and did express outrage over actions taken against blacks. But they combined it with constitutional interpretations that denied these victims federal protection—the one factor that was crucial in their fight for equality.

Even in 1896, however, some Americans realized that the present could not bind the future. The prestigious *American Law Review* took note of Harlan's dissent. True enough, the majority opinion "is in accordance with the analogies of other decisions both in the Federal and the State tribunals." But Harlan's dissent, "whatever may be thought of it now, will do him honor in the estimation of future generations, who will study with curiosity these statutes, which will have become dead letters."[32] Indeed, in 1866 supporters of the new Fourteenth Amendment had noted its potential for *future* change. Thaddeus Stevens argued for its adoption "because it is all that can be obtained in the present state of public opinion. . . . I will take all I can get . . . and leave it to be perfected by better men in better times. It may be that that time will not come while I am here to enjoy the glorious triumph; but that it will come is as certain as that there is a just God."[33] Stevens realized that nothing is permanent in legal interpetation. One could only wonder when the *full* force of the amendment would be realized, if indeed it ever could be.

Most of its later progress in this direction would come after 1920. By the end of the nineteenth century, however, the Fourteenth Amendment had enjoyed great success in another area. Given the importance that it has assumed today for civil liberties, one may be surprised to learn that its late-nineteenth-century primacy had little, if any, relevance to this topic.

---

[31] *United States v. Cruikshank,* 92 U.S. 542, 552, 554–555 (1875).
[32] *American Law Review,* 30 (1896), 785.
[33] Bickel, "Original Understanding," pp. 45–46.

Munn v. Illinois (1876)

No one denied that the new amendment both protected a citizen's rights and defined citizenship in the first place. But which rights did it protect? Certainly not the freedoms we associate with the Bill of Rights, for they were not held applicable to the states until after 1920. Rather, it was a more subtle and general form of rights that the amendment appeared to secure. Lawyers for the butchers hinted at the new category in *Slaughter-House* in 1873, and another lawyer expanded the point in an important case *(Munn v. Illinois)* three years later.[34] However, it was not until 1890 that the Supreme Court gave full expression to the general area of protection called *due process.*

In *Slaughter-House,* lawyers for the plaintiffs had argued that due process, for them at least, meant the right to pursue whatever lawful calling they wished to undertake, unhampered by such restrictions as those imposed by the Louisiana legislature. In other words, they claimed to be protected from "improper" or "arbitrary" or "unreasonable" regulation. Further, they insisted that with the new amendment, additional security was to be given them—more than would have been the case prior to the amendment's adoption. Since there was no doubt that the Fourteenth Amendment applied to the states, what might have been permissible before 1868 was now forbidden. It became the job of the courts, especially the federal courts, to make sure that the states did not transcend their lawful authority.

As we have seen, the Court rejected this viewpoint by a 1-vote majority in 1873. But three years later it had to confront the same argument, only this time the issue involved grain elevator owners, not butchers.

By the late nineteenth century, farmers (who still considered themselves the backbone of American society) were increasingly unhappy. Industrial changes, which occurred with such rapidity in the post–Civil War era, had significantly affected their way of life. New mechanical harvesting made it possible to plant and gather hundreds of thousands more bushels of grain than had been true in the 1850s. And the railroad, together with the development of grain storage facilities known as elevators, and a modern system of grain marketing known as futures trading, tended to leave the "independent yeoman" a prisoner of

[34] *Munn v. Illinois,* 94 U.S. 113 (1877).

the new industrial "progress." When a railroad joined forces with a particular elevator, agreeing for example not to store any grain unless it was carried by cars of that particular railroad, farmers, who depended on the railroad as their only means of getting the grain into the elevators, had no choice but to pay whatever the railroad charged. Unless the grain was placed in storage where it could await transportation to the milling centers, the grain would rot. Other businessmen suffering from the collusion between railroad and elevator operators joined agrarian protests, and the result in the Midwest was a series of statutes known as Granger Laws, enacted generally between 1868 and 1875.

Typical of such laws was one passed in Illinois. It stipulated the amount of money that a grain elevator operator could charge for storing grain and provided penalties if these rates were exceeded. One owner of a large elevator (who also had been expelled from the Chicago Board of Trade for dishonesty) was found guilty of violating the law and appealed to the courts to have the measure declared unconstitutional. The United States Supreme Court decided the case of *Munn v. Illinois* in 1876.

Ira Munn's lawyer argued that while it would have been highly inappropriate under any conditions for the legislature to pass such a statute, it was absolutely unthinkable now that the Fourteenth Amendment had become part of the Constitution (see Documents, pp. 126-131). The attorney general for Illinois did not spend a great deal of time on the Fourteenth Amendment at all but simply noted the holding in *Slaughter-House.* "we insist," he wrote, that under the Fourteenth Amendment it cannot "be held that the act in question deprives warehousemen of their property without due process of law, although its prescribes the maximum rates which may be charged for the storage of grain by those following the vocation of public warehousemen." All that the law did was to ensure "that if [a warehouseman] uses his property for a specific purpose, and follows the vocation of a public warehouseman, he shall conform to certain regulations deemed essential to the protection of public interests." Indeed, he was not "required by law to use his property for the storage of grain for the public, nor in any wise to follow the vocation of a public warehouseman."[35]

The Court, by a vote of 7 to 2, agreed. "When private property is devoted to a public use, it is subject to public regulation." If the owner's property is devoted to a use in which there is a public interest, "he, in

---

[35] "Brief for Appellee" in *Landmark Briefs and Arguments of the Supreme Court of the United States,* vol. 7, pp. 632-633. See also pp. 636-646.

effect, grants to the public an interest in that use, and must submit to be controlled by the public for the common good, to the extent of the interest he has thus created. He may withdraw the grant by discontinuing the use." As for the tendency for legislatures to misuse their lawmaking authority, Chief Justice Waite concluded that "for protection against abuses by legislatures the people must resort to the polls, not to the courts."[36] Justice Field dissented, calling the principles on which the majority based the decision "subversive of the rights of private property." He relied heavily on the Fourteenth Amendment as a barrier against the statute passed in Illinois (see Documents, pp. 131–134).

Although Field may not have been aware of it, the fact is that the Court had shifted much closer to his position in the three years since *Slaughter-House.* In *Munn,* the Court made no mention whatsoever of all the limiting characteristics of the Fourteenth Amendment that it had earlier deemed so important, such as its history and the obvious intent that it was to apply primarily to the ex-slave. At no point does Chief Justice Waite even hint that it was improper for *Munn* to cite the Fourteenth Amendment, although Munn was no more an ex-slave than any of the butchers had been. However, even though Munn lost his case, in that the Court sustained the Illinois statute, the judges may well have accepted his major premise: that the Fourteenth Amendment banned certain kinds of state-imposed regulations concerning private business enterprise.

The Minnesota Rate Case (1890)

In 1890, the Field viewpoint captured a majority of the Supreme Court justices, including Justice Miller, author of the original *Slaughter-House* opinion seventeen years before. Old and ill, Miller probably had yet to comprehend the magnitude of the new interpretation given the Fourteenth Amendment. He concurred in the decision "with some hesitation." Again a regulatory statute enacted by a state was involved, and again the plaintiffs (in this case the Chicago, Milwaukee and St. Paul Railway Company) argued that the law deprived the railroad of its property without due process of law. In 1887, Minnesota adopted legislation establishing a railroad and warehouse commission, which could determine the maximum a railroad could charge for hauling

[36] *Munn v. Illinois,* 94. U.S. 113, 126, 130 (1877).

freight within the state. Once the commission had determined what rate was reasonable, the railroad had no choice but to charge those rates. Further, the statute appeared to give the railroad no opportunity to take the matter to court if it disagreed with the ruling of the commission. (See Documents, pp. 137–139.)

The briefs filed by opposing lawyers in this case illustrate once again that law is a response to various pressures and stresses within a society. By 1889–1890 social tensions in America were increasing. Midwestern farmer protests as well as major labor unrest had become noticeable. Conservatives in business, as well as on the bench and of the bar, pointed toward "socialist" legislation being forced through quiescent state legislatures by well-organized pressure groups. Now, more than ever, it seemed imperative that the courts (especially the federal courts—because their judges were appointed, whereas most state judges were elected) stand fast as a bulwark protecting the rights of property from the wrongs of disorder, confiscation, and unwarranted legislative interference with basic rights.

On behalf of its new railroad commission, the state of Minnesota filed a brief of less than fourteen pages, relying heavily on *Munn*. Noting that several other cases since *Munn* had followed the earlier decision, the commission argued that "the question of the reasonableness of the rate is a question for legislative determination, and when so determined, ceases to be the subject of judicial scrutiny." Further, in virtually all the cases dealing with this type of statute, the Supreme Court had approved the enactments even though they actually set rates that the railroads were compelled to follow. Indeed, "this principle has become too firmly established to be overthrown."[37]

The two briefs filed on behalf of the railroad came to over 150 pages. Too shrewd to ask the Court directly to overrule *Munn,* the lawyers sought instead to discredit the holding indirectly. One attorney, for example, insisted that prior to *Munn* "the history of either English or American legislation or jurisprudence furnishes no authority for the exercise of any such power by the State." In other words, *Munn* should be regarded as an aberration, a freak that should never have happened. The statute that it approved "is destructive of the rights of property and more to be feared than the insane ravings of the advocates of socialism and the commune." A second technique used in the brief was to describe in graphic terms the implications if *Munn* was not overruled.

[37] *Chicago, Milwaukee and St. Paul Railway Co. v. Minnesota,* 134 U.S. 418 (1890), *Brief for Appellee,* pp. 11, 14 (on file Harvard Law School Library).

Thus the lawyer quoted Chief Justice Waite's famous conclusion that "for protection against abuses the people must resort to the polls." He then claimed that by such a decision, "the entire railroad property of the United States is handed over to the government and control of the Legislatures of the several States ... without control from the Courts, and it is distinctly announced that any injustice perpetrated must be righted by an appeal to the people at the polls." This could result only in the railroads being compelled "to take part in every election, and exercise their influence to secure the selection of representatives favorable to their interests," making the railroads in a real sense "part of the spoils of the contest." Virtually admitting to the judges that the railroads would be responsible for much of the corruption that would inevitably result, the lawyer reminded the court that "the owners and managers of railroads are only human and it is too much to expect that they will stand idly by and see their property despoiled and their investments ruined, if by any means it can be prevented." All these evils, he insisted, flowed from the doctrine of *Munn,* a doctrine in reality "against public morals as well as public policy."[38]

The other attorney for the railroad asked the court to consider the implications of the statute sustained by the Supreme Court of Minnesota. It permitted the commission to be the *final* judges of what was reasonable in terms of rates. However, "it is always a judicial question as to whether a statute is repugnant to provisions of the constitution of ... the United States." Again, the unasked question becomes important. Given the tenor of the times, did the judges really wish to abdicate their right of involvement in the legislative process, as the Minnesota Supreme Court appeared to have done? Fully conceding the public right to secure for the public reasonable railroad charges for transportation, the railroad denied "its right to arbitrarily and finally fix or determine such charges by positive statute, and most respectfully [asked] Your Honors to again review" the *Munn* decision.[39]

By a vote of 6 to 3, the United States Supreme Court declared the statute as interpreted by Minnesota's highest court to be unconstitutional (see Documents, pp. 140–142). It neither cited nor mentioned *Munn.* In sharp dissent, however, Justice Bradley complained bitterly that the decision practically overruled *Munn* (see Documents, pp. 142–145). Like *Plessy v. Ferguson,* the Minnesota Rate case represents an important step in the Court's treatment of the Fourteenth Amend-

[38] Ibid., *Brief for Appellants,* #1; pp. 23, 47–48, 49.
[39] Ibid., *Brief for Appellants,* #2; p. 45.

ment. With this decision, the justices served notice that they, and presumably other courts as well, would now have the last word about being deprived of property without due process of law. In the rate case, the court insisted that what was "reasonable" was ultimately a judicial question. From here, it soon advanced to the process of actually having to compute, in later cases, what it considered a reasonable rate of return. Numerous critics of the Court during the late nineteenth century objected to the justices' use of the Fourteenth Amendment as a shield for judicial intervention. In recent years, contemporary observers of the Court have objected to the same tendency, particularly since 1954. Courts reflect their times, just as the law they interpret ultimately reflects the society from which it comes. The Fourteenth Amendment remains today what it was in 1868, a constitutional provision whose potential *both* for progress and for regression continues to be very strong.

Law and Economic Growth: Courts, Corporations, and Constitutional Doctrines

The Fourteenth Amendment did more than transform the relationship between the state and the citizen. It affected the basic economic instrument by which the United States expanded during the nineteenth century—the corporate charter. By the time of the Revolution, the charter had come to be regarded as an imperial tool with which to nurture British rule. In the wake of American independence, the corporation evolved from an artificial concept to a legal person. Although there was no doubt that either Congress or the state legislatures could grant corporate charters, until the Jacksonian period charters were generally the exception, not the rule.

A charter implied a monopoly, and hostility toward monopolies in general lay deep within American legal history. Objections to the East India tea monopoly, for example, played a not unimportant role in nurturing prerevolutionary opposition to the British Empire. However, if the public clearly benefited from the monopoly, and if the activity could not be undertaken at all except by the private sector, American public policy encouraged such ventures. See the comments on this point by Chief Justice Marshall in the *Dartmouth College* case (*Dartmouth College v. Woodward,* 4 Wheaton 518 [1819]). While these distinctions may have been important in 1819, by the 1830s they had lessened, even as the rate of incorporation expanded.

One scholar notes that by 1830, about 1,900 corporations had been chartered in New England alone. In 1836–1837, New York incorporated "almost 200 companies, Ohio over 150, Pennsylvania more than 100."[1]

---

[1] Abram Chayes, "Introduction," in John P. Davis, *Corporations* (1961), pp. vii–viii.

In truth, corporations had "arrived" on the American scene even before Jackson became President. However, they were now no longer regarded as quasi-public institutions, with their primary purpose intended to benefit the public interest. To block further creation of charters would be to endorse the exclusive privileges and elitism that the Jacksonians were now challenging. Hence charter privileges should be available to all who sought them.

Far from showing hostility to corporations, it was the Jacksonians who, to paraphrase Arthur Schlesinger, Jr., sprinkled holy water on them, cleansed them of the legal taint of monopoly, and sent them forth "as the benevolent agents of free competition."[2] It was the Jacksonians who, in the name of antimonopoly, laid the foundations for the corporate monopolies of the post–Civil War industrial era. All that the Jacksonians lacked was an effective tool with which to balance the "public interest" against the rights of corporate enterprises to the security of their invested expectations. This instrument was ultimately provided by the generation of leaders who matured during the heady Jacksonian era—specifically, the framers of the Fourteenth Amendment. Holding that corporations were entitled to the protection of life, liberty, and property afforded to all by the new amendment completed the circle begun with the great increase in charters in the 1830s.

Transformation of the Corporation

For the most part, the corporations that would seek protection from the new amendment were very different from the late-eighteenth-century models. One obvious change was in the amount of money needed to capitalize large corporate ventures. In 1910, for example, the book value of the Standard Oil Company was more than $600 million, and in 1901 the newly created U.S. Steel Corporation began its corporate life with a capitalization figure of over $1 billion. These huge amounts of required capital made the Jacksonian concept of corporate privileges—as something readily available for everyone—anachronistic, if not totally inaccurate. Furthermore, the corporations increasingly reflected a new separation between ownership and management.

In the earlier period, corporations had been built by families, who were intimately involved with their operations. Once large numbers of

[2] Ibid., p. ix.

stockholders were involved, it became virtually impossible for the small owner to retain direction. This tendency to fragment ownership into shares resulted in what one scholar has called "ownership diluted."[3] Ownership now no longer necessarily implied control of corporate operations. Indeed, inability to affect important business decisions sometimes led to the failure of shareholders to protect themselves against adverse policies, to say nothing of manipulation or mismanagement. By the late nineteenth century, and with no sense of inconsistency, many shareholders—the "offspring" of the self-reliant, risk-taking Jacksonians—called for state regulation in the "public interest." They wanted "a remedy against speculative directors and managers, some provision against an impairment of their investment . . . a guarantee against unfair leases . . . or other arrangements made by directors without the consent of stockholders. . . . In a word, merchants want to be protected against the railroads, the railroads want to be protected against themselves, and investors against both. And they all cry for the same soothing syrup—legislative enactment."[4]

These grievances, however, resulted at least in part from the remarkable increase in corporate activity after the Civil War. Public policy facilitated such increases, both in the size of corporations and in their numbers, by the enactment of statutes that made it very easy to incorporate. (See, for example, Documents, pp. 145–149.) Statutes of this type reflected again the Jacksonian bias that corporate creation should be common practice, not class privilege. When one adds the use of trusts and holding companies, the issuance of preferred stock, and other devices that appeared to be part of corporate expansion, it seems that American public policy balanced industrial power heavily in favor of the larger firms. On the other hand, growing pressure for some sort of regulation could not be denied.

Origins of Administrative Agencies

Public policy accepted such developments as industrialism, combination and monopoly, and technology while at the same time seeking to keep some sort of order, even as those vast changes took place. It had become obvious by the post–Civil War era that state legislatures were ill

---

[3] Ibid., p. xviii.
[4] Quoted in Lee Benson, *Merchants, Farmers & Railroads* (1955), p. 204.

equipped to offer direct and effective supervision of activities concerning railroads and warehouses, sanitation, and public health—areas that had become through necessity, not foresight, subjects for legislative attention. In this period, however, most state legislatures met for a term ranging from a few weeks to a few months, sometimes annually, sometimes every other year. This fact, itself a reflection of a long popular ideal of limited government, made day-to-day supervision of such activities impossible. Similarly state courts, with their formal structure and inability to anticipate problems in public policy on a continual basis, were equally ill suited for this task. Yet day-to-day, ongoing supervision of corporate enterprise such as railroads was essential if the regulation now demanded in the name of the public interest was to be effective.

The late-nineteenth-century response to this challenge was a hybrid governmental institution that combined executive, legislative, and judicial responsibilities. From the late 1860s to the present, the proliferation of regulatory commissions, also known as administrative law agencies, has continued, so that they are now sometimes referred to as the fourth branch of government. Two general characteristics of regulatory commissions, or administrative agencies, should be noted.

First, these bodies are separate from both the legislature and the courts. Yet they legislate, in that they adopt regulations; and they adjudicate, in that they hold hearings and render quasi-judicial opinions. They are also separate from the executive branch, although their members are usually appointed either by the governor or, in the case of a federal regulatory commission, by the President. Like other parts of an executive branch, they attempt to enforce the appropriate law. Thus regulatory agencies can supervise, legislate, investigate, adjudicate, prosecute, negotiate, and issue findings of fact. In the period under discussion they seemed well equipped to provide the continuous monitoring of a railroad or grain elevator or similar type of business.

Second, these bodies receive authority to act through delegation. They are creations of legislatures, from which they receive, through appropriate statutes, their legal authority to act. They serve on behalf of the legislature and the courts, which have delegated certain responsibilities, such as those just mentioned. Delegation, however, has long troubled certain critics of public policy, who see it as a dangerous departure from the separation of powers. As late as 1892, two years after the Minnesota Rate case, the United States Supreme Court declared: "that Congress cannot delegate legislative power ... is a principle universally recognized as vital to the integrity and maintenance of ... government ordained by the Constitution."[5]

Delegation to commissions had occurred extensively long before 1892 in both state and nation, with the Court's acquiescence if not its approbation. However, invariably the railroads or other interests seeking to challenge a regulatory statute would, in their efforts to show the law as beyond the power of the legislature, invoke the doctrine of improper delegation. Thus an unequivocal judicial acceptance of the doctrine of delegation was extremely important. If state regulatory statutes were declared unconstitutional because of improper delegation, the entire embryonic structure of administrative regulation would be in jeopardy—which brings us back to the Minnesota Rate case. The most important aspect of the case for the Minnesota Supreme Court was this question of delegation. The justices unanimously affirmed the right of the legislature to delegate some authority to smaller groups.[6] The fact that the United States Supreme Court reversed the decision on totally different grounds should not obscure the significance of the lower decision for administrative regulation.

In examining the Minnesota statute, one should notice the extensive authority granted the railroad commission. (See Documents, pp. 137–139.) Indeed, it may well have been the apparent inability of the law to reconcile open-ended regulatory authority with the right of court intervention that rendered the enactment unacceptable to the Court. There were, however, other regulatory models available. In 1869, for example, Massachusetts established a railroad commission, and its functions and powers should be contrasted with those of Minnesota. (See Documents, pp. 134–137.) The man generally credited with having secured legislative approval for the Massachusetts commission was Charles Francis Adams, Jr., a member of one of the most famous American families. Adams was appointed a commissioner almost immediately after the act became effective, and he remained on the board for ten years, usually serving as its chairman. Like the other Adamses, he was a prolific writer, and his comments on railroad regulation offer insights not only into the peculiar course railroad regulation took but also into the perennial tensions within the regulatory process.

[5] *Field v. Clark*, 143 U.S. 649, 692 (1892).
[6] *State ex. rel. Commission v. Chicago, Milwaukee and St. Paul Railway*, 38 Minn. 281 (1888).

Looking back on his years as a Massachusetts railroad commissioner, Adams noted that American railroads had been built on a tragic error: the assumption that "in all matters of trade, competition, if allowed perfectly free play, could be relied upon to protect the community from abuses."[7] Instead, lack of foresight and planning, coupled with haphazard financial arrangements, led to the proliferation of railroads, and the result was a chaotic and inefficient transportation system. Even worse, according to Adams, was the fact that "the railroads had been built much too rapidly, and the business of the country could not support them. Those immediately in charge were under a constant and severe pressure to earn money, and they earned it whenever and however they could. They stopped at nothing. Between those years (1866 and 1873) it is safe to say that the idea of any duty that a railroad corporation owed to the public was wholly lost sight of."[8] Popular resentment against the "gross financial scandals," which disgraced the management of many railroads, increased the demands for public regulation. "The system was, indeed, fairly honeycombed with jobbery and corruption."[9] Note Jay Gould's famous comment about corruption and the Erie railroad: "It was the custom when men received nominations to come to me for contributions, and I made them and considered them good paying investments for the company; in a republican district I was a strong republican, in a democratic district, I was democratic, and in doubtful districts I was doubtful; in politics, I was an Erie railroad man every time."[10]

Adams believed that the "arrogant and singularly injudicious" attitude that the railroads displayed toward the growing supporters of governmental regulation made a bad scene even worse. "They practically undertook to set even public opinion at defiance."[11] The result was state regulation on a widespread scale, followed by federal intervention of a sort beginning in 1887. While the arrogant attitudes of the railroads may have helped bring on regulation, the form such regulation took was also flawed. Adams observed that "the inclination of the American mind is not bureaucratic." Public policy, he wrote, turns "to commissions, as our bureaus are called, with great reluctance." Writing with that sense of icy detachment—again typical of the Adams family, especially after the

[7] Charles Francis Adams, Jr., *Railroads: Their Origins and Problems* (1893), p. 117.
[8] Ibid., p. 123.
[9] Ibid., p. 126.
[10] Benson, *Merchants,* p. 62.
[11] Adams, *Railroads,* p. 127.

Civil War—and neglecting to mention that he himself had not only been instrumental in the creation of such a commission but had been its leading figure for ten years, Adams concluded that this distrust was well deserved: "As a rule, they do not work well...even when honestly composed, they rarely accomplish much. Once created, also, they can never be gotten rid of."[12]

These criticisms were compounded by an inability to select commissioners with any substantial knowledge of railroading. Here Adams conveniently ignored the key question: outside of the railroad themselves, where was such expertise available, and was it desirable to use personnel drawn from the railroads to staff a supposedly independent public regulatory commission designed to regulate the railroads themselves?[13] Finally, Adams insisted that the most serious weakness in the still young American pattern of regulatory commissions lay in the misconceptions held by those appointed to them. All too often, commissioners "reflected the angry complexion of the movement out of which they had originated." They should have expected—and have been expected—to investigate serious problems arising from railroad operation, and then to propose appropriate solutions. Instead, "they were there to prosecute. The test of their performance...was to be sought in the degree of hostility they manifested to the railroad corporations. In a word, they represented force."[14]

Under these circumstances, Adams found it remarkable not that the railroad commissions failed to achieve complete success but rather that they succeeded at all. "That they did succeed was due solely to the incorrigible folly and passionate love of fighting which seems inherent in the trained American railroad official." This was all the more unfortunate, he wrote, because there was another choice available, namely the Massachusetts Act of 1869. To the extent that the Massachusetts commission succeeded, it was not because it had the power to set rates (the law deliberately declined to give the new commission such authority, and under Adams's leadership the members steadfastly refused to seek it) but because the commission served "as a sort of lens by means of which the otherwise scattered rays of public opinion could be

---

[12] Ibid., p. 132.
[13] Put another way, the problem raised here is simply how to protect the regulators from becoming subservient to the very interests they are supposed to regulate. See Thomas K. McCraw, "Regulation in America: A Review Article," *Business History Review,* 49 (1975), 150-183; also Jonathan Lurie, *The Chicago Board of Trade 1859-1905: The Dynamics of Self-Regulation* (1979), chap. 1.
[14] Adams, *Railroads,* p. 125.

concentrated to focus and brought to bear upon a given point." Indeed, the commissioners "had to listen, and they might investigate and report—they could do little more." If the statute worked, and Adams modestly concluded that it did, this was because the law rested "on the one great social feature which distinguishes modern civilization from any other of which we have a record—the eventual supremacy of an enlightened public opinion."[15]

In retrospect, Adams seems to have been naive in his confidence in the potency of public opinion. While he knew that railroads could not base their rates on competition, he was unable to provide a viable alternative to external rate regulation. Invariably his first step would be the exhaustive collection of data concerning costs. But the next step eluded him. Ambivalent in his attitude toward regulation in general, unable to reconcile rates, railroads, and political realities, by 1878 Adams was writing of his service on the commission: "How wearisome all this is! Can I ever get rid of this beastly Commissionership!"[16] It might be some small consolation to Adams were he to learn that more than one century after the Massachusetts law was passed, effective railroad regulation matched with efficient railroad operation remains a goal, not a reality.

Although the years after the Civil War had signaled the modern era of industrialization with its necessity for state regulation, public policy also tended to encourage private regulatory activity. Perhaps this was because it was a more familiar pattern to the American legal order; possibly it was because it seemed to show that basically American society had not changed in the years since 1865. While in some cases, notably the commodities exchanges, private regulation may have been effective, in general its benefits were very mixed.[17] Reliance on the private sector aided by beneficent use of law certainly stimulated railroads, corporate enterprise, and modern factories, replete with trusts, monopolies, and so forth. Indeed, these institutions matured virtually free from government interference, if not interest. There was no central planning, no systematic allocation of either industrial or natural resources. And when the inevitable public pressure mounted for some sort of governmental intervention, the subjects to be regulated were themselves powerful and institutionalized, making the prospects of effective state regulation dubious at best. On the other hand, public

---

[15] Ibid., p. 140.
[16] Edward C. Kirkland, *Charles Francis Adams, Jr.* (1965), pp. 56–57.
[17] Lurie, *Chicago Board of Trade*, chap. 8

policy also failed to make the best use of effective private regulation. The result was a continuing tension between private regulatory patterns and public regulatory agencies. The late nineteenth century failed to resolve this tension, and whether the twentieth century would do better was equally uncertain as the United States entered the World War I era.

The Sherman Act and Antitrust Litigation

During the late nineteenth century, even as regulatory commissions were established, the alternative of direct legislative action always remained. In one very important area, Congress chose not to delegate at first but rather to enact a regulatory statute. The early federal policy toward antitrust legislation further illustrates the ambivalence with which Americans have regarded competition, cooperation, and corporate growth, as well as their perhaps excessive confidence in the magical powers of legislation.

The discussion of the Fourteenth Amendment with which this essay started indicated how difficult a question concerning the meanings of words and the intentions of the framers could become. The Sherman Antitrust Act, enacted in 1890 and still the foundation for all major federal antitrust activity, while demonstrating anew this difficulty, is significant for another reason as well. It reveals a unique American faith in statutory relief. William Letwin has commented about the typical American view that social problems can be resolved simply by another statute. The public perceives a problem; it protests; the elected representatives respond with a statute that solves the problem; and the process soon begins all over again. He argues that this pattern rests on two important assumptions: (1) that both the public and the legislature have a *clear* understanding of what is wrong and (2) that the legislature is able to resolve the difficulty by finding the appropriate words for a statute that can correct it.[18] Both assumptions, as far as Letwin is concerned, are problematical, if not actually wrong.

More often than not, the truth seems to be that the public is unable to identify the actual cause of its unhappiness, while the legislature may have equal difficulty, once it has perceived what appears to be the cause, in providing statutory relief. Further, a statute is not self-executing; it requires interpretation both by those who must act under it—such as

[18] William Letwin, *Law and Economic Policy in America* (1965), pp. v–vi.

federal officials—and by those ultimately charged with deciding the proper scope of the law, if not its basic constitutionality—the courts. It must be emphasized, however, that there is enough truth in the oversimplified discontent–pressure–statute syndrome to suggest caution before disregarding it. What people believe to be true may on occasion be more important in bringing about legal change than what actually turns out to be the case.

We have already noted the major role that antimonopoly sentiment played in eighteenth- and early-nineteenth-century American history, to say nothing of the Midwestern agrarian agitation that led to the Granger Laws and *Munn v. Illinois.* Thus, the Sherman act of 1890 could be seen as merely the latest manifestation of a longstanding antipathy toward monopolistic tendencies. The very dramatic increase in large corporate structures between 1860 and 1890 within a context of burgeoning factories and urban growth simply brought home as never before the potential power inherent in business combinations. Although to what extent is not clear, equal opportunity did remain a proclaimed goal during the late nineteenth century.

There was, however, another side to consider. American public policy, even as it condemned monopoly, encouraged economic growth, of which consolidation and expansion were inevitable and often praiseworthy aspects. The legal order deliberately used law to facilitate what has been described as "the release of energy."[19] Indeed, the active role of government in promoting economic productivity through such devices as general incorporation laws, land grants, favorable tariffs, or laws that limited liability was widely understood and accepted, if not actively discussed. One should also remember the evolutionary doctrines current during this period. Whether such ideas as survival of the fittest or the inevitability of successful corporate enterprise were accurate is less important than the fact that they were widely held to be accurate. What, after all, was a trust if not proof that one had truly succeeded in one's particular business calling?

In short, both a fear *of* competition and a fear *for* competition were important factors in bringing about the Sherman Antitrust Act. How could a statute be worded that would (1) not impede individual effort, (2) encourage economic growth, (3) discourage "undesirable" monopolies, and (4) not interfere with "reasonable" competition? The answer for public policy in 1890 was, of course, the Sherman Act, which Letwin

[19] J. Willard Hurst, *Law and the Conditions of Freedom in the Nineteenth Century United States* (1956).

calls "as good an antitrust law as the Congress of 1890 could have devised."[20] (See Documents, pp. 149-150.)

Athough the key sections of the act are only two sentences long, they are very ambiguous. What did the framers intend? While there are some points that can be made in answering this question, it remains the wrong question to ask. Here again, the key issues should be not what the framers intended but what they wrote into the statute and what those words meant both to contemporary observers and to subsequent judges. There was no doubt that the federal government could intervene directly in the organization of economic life. It had been doing so since the Federalist era. Nor was there any doubt that public policy as well as contemporary legal understanding of the common law opposed monopoly in general. Moreover, since 68 members of the Senate out of 82 were lawyers, it must be assumed that the vast majority were familiar with accepted legal interpetations of such terms as a "monopoly" or "combination."

The new statute, which passed in the Senate 52 to 1 and in the House by voice vote, forbade trusts, combinations, and contracts "in restraint of trade." But could a trust exist at all without being in restraint of trade? To put it another way, was a trust or monopoly in and of itself a restraint of trade? Did the statute ban all trusts, combinations, or monopolies, or just those combinations, contracts, and trusts "in restraint of trade"? It seems certain that the framers did not intend to block *all* combinations. Their inability to be more precise as to what types of business actions they did intend to prohibit led them to adopt the very flexible language that appears in the law. Nevertheless, the key author of the Sherman Act (not, incidentally, Senator Sherman but rather Senator George Edmunds of Vermont) claimed that the measure was a "bill that is clear in its terms, is definite in its definitions, and is broad in its comprehension, without winding it up into infinite details."[21]

Although some states, such as Massachusetts, require their state supreme court to render advisory opinions in response to questions of law put to it by the other branches of government, the United States Supreme Court has consistently declined to follow such a course, insisting that the issue to be resolved must arise from "an actual case or controversy." This practice, while it may say much for the separation of powers doctrine, has some drawbacks. It leaves federal legislators a little uncertain as to how their work will fare in the courts. Further, knowing

---

[20] Letwin, *Law and Economic Policy,* p. 95.
[21] Ibid.

that a statute may be challenged in court, congressmen may be more inclined to include provisions in the law that they assume will be thrown out by the courts—resulting in the legislatures avoiding their own responsibilities, and the courts perhaps assuming responsibility where they should not. Those who voted for the Sherman Act realized that they were enacting an "experimental" statute, one based on "general principles." Rightly or wrongly, they also fully expected the courts to refine and delineate the actual perimeters of what was permissible under the law and what practices it forbade.

Although detailed analysis of the varied treatment the Sherman Antitrust Act has had at the hands of the courts is beyond the scope of this essay, three Supreme Court cases ought to be mentioned. The first, the *E.C. Knight* case of 1895, is significant because it represents the initial attempt by the Court to determine what the statute meant—at least to the judges! The second is the Northern Securities Company case of 1904, in which Justice Holmes delivered one of his most famous dissents, setting forth again the continuing dilemma with which federal antitrust policy is confronted. The third is the *Standard Oil* case of 1911, in which the Court articulated the "rule of reason" doctrine, and in which Justice Harlan offered some noteworthy observations about judicial legislation that still have significance for understanding the way in which the Court can interact with other branches of government.

The *Knight* case involved the consolidation of several sugar manufacturing plants within one parent trust. Because the justices found no legal necessity for invoking the Sherman Act, the decision has sometimes been regarded as an example of a conservative, nit-picking Court, bending over backwards to protect "big business." It may well be, however, that such is not an accurate perception. All four plants involved in the "deal" that the government sought to have canceled were lcoated not only wthin the same state but also within the same city (Philadelphia). But the Sherman Act condemned combinations "in restraint of trade or commerce among the several states." In terms of manufacturing sugar, there seemed little doubt that interstate commerce was not involved.

Did the Sherman Act apply to a monopoly involving manufacture, as opposed to commerce? In answering no to this question, Chief Justice Fuller indicated that the government had focused on manufacture when it should have emphasized the effect such manufacturing arrangements would have on interstate commerce. Given the fact that Fuller did not appear impressed with the business activities of the sugar trust, it may well be that had the government focused on restraints to interstate commerce, the decision might have been in its favor. If the *Knight* decision is a "conservative" opinion, it is because the Court refused to go beyond the interpretation of the facts argued by the government. Moreover, the decision "did not lay down the rule... that manufacturers as such are immune from the Sherman act, but rather held that manufacturing was immune, and therefore, that manufacturers were subject to the act only insofar as their activities constituted interstate commerce or directly affected it."[22] (See Documents, pp. 151–155.)

The 1904 *Northern Securities* case featured several of the most famous (or infamous) names in late-nineteenth century high finance: James J. Hill, J.P. Morgan, and E.H. Harriman. At stake was the control of the three major railroads in the western half of the United States: the Great Northern, the Northern Pacific, and the Burlington. Through a very complicated set of financial dealings, replete with melodramatic twists and turns, late in 1901 Hill and Morgan established the three railroads as one huge integrated system, the largest holding company yet known in the United States. The venture was publicly announced about two months after Theodore Roosevelt had become President, following the assassination of William McKinley on September 6, 1901. Early in 1902, the federal government intervened against the Northern Securities Company on direct instructions from the new President.

Why Roosevelt sought to challenge Hill and Morgan so soon after taking office is not clear. His own philosophy toward monopoly was somewhat nebulous. He believed that antitrust laws were ineffective and that publicity was a very potent weapon against "bad" trusts. He further claimed that states could resolve trust problems on their own but that federal intervention would be a feasible alternative if necessary. Perhaps the new President wanted to use the Northern Securities case as an example on which to build a stronger antitrust policy that would have popular support. At any rate, in 1904 the United States Supreme Court, in a 5-to-4 ruling, supported the government's viewpoint and ordered the holding company dissolved. But the case is notable not so much for the majority opinion as for one of its two dissents, that written by a new member of the Court, Mr. Justice Holmes.

Oliver Wendell Holmes, Jr., the son of a well-known New England doctor and literary figure, had already distinguished himself as a

[22] Ibid., pp. 165–166.

member and later as chief justice of the Massachusetts Supreme Judicial Court. President Roosevelt was much impressed by certain of Holmes's decisions in labor cases, such as *Vegelahn v. Guntner* (1896), in which Holmes objected strongly to the use of injunctions as an antiunion device. When Mr. Justice Gray, also from Massachusetts, retired within a year after Roosevelt became President, Holmes seemed a natural choice. Yet Roosevelt appeared to have had some doubts. In a revealing letter to Henry Cabot Lodge, Republican senator from Massachusetts and a leading supporter of Holmes's appointment as well as one of Roosevelt's closest friends, Roosevelt wrote of the proposed nominee, "I should naturally expect him to be in favor of those principles in which I so earnestly believe."

> In the ordinary and low sense which we attach to the words "partisan" and "politician," a judge of the Supreme Court should be neither. But in the higher sense, in the proper sense, he is not in my judgment fitted for the position unless he is a party man, a constructive statesman, constantly keeping in mind his adherence to the principles and policies under which this nation has been built up ... and keeping in mind also his relations with his fellow statesmen who in other branches of the government are striving in cooperation with him to advance the ends of government.[23]

Roosevelt's feelings are of interest if only because few Presidents have taken the time to set down their ideas as to the criteria for the type of judicial appointment they seek to make. Obviously he was satisfied about Holmes because he appointed the Massachusetts jurist to the bench, confident that they both agreed on the need to distinguish "good" trusts from "bad" trusts and that Holmes would surely find for the government in its efforts to break up the Northern Securities Company. Like Presidents before and since, Roosevelt was to learn to his sorrow that past beliefs are no sure indication of future judicial attitudes. Although the Court upheld Roosevelt by one vote, his first appointee, the man to whom he had so confidently looked for support, voted against him.

Holmes's dissent (see Documents, pp. 156–159) is generally regarded as one of his finest efforts: lucid and at the same time tantalizing. It is significant because better than most judges before him, Holmes confronted the very difficult task of reconciling two divergent aims of

[23] Henry Cabot Lodge, *Selections from the Correspondence of Theodore Roosevelt and Henry Cabot Lodge* (1925), p. 518.

American antitrust policy that have been there from its beginnings. By adopting a statute that the courts would ultimately have to interpret, Congress sought "to preserve the benefits of competition while enjoying the benefits of consolidation."[24] Unless, therefore, Congress intended to break up every combination (an impossible conclusion according to Holmes), he failed to see how the Northern Securities Company had violated the Sherman Act. Certainly the legislature had not planned to enact a statute that would "disintegrate society so far as it could into individual atoms."

Privately, Holmes believed that the Sherman Act was "a humbug, based on economic ignorance and incompetence." Roosevelt, for his part, concluded after Holmes's dissent that "I could carve out of a banana a judge with more backbone than that!"[25] Two years after the case, Roosevelt wrote to Lodge that "nothing has been so strongly borne in on me concerning lawyers on the bench as that the *nominal* politics of a man has nothing to do with his actions on the bench. His *real* politics are all important . . . , Holmes should have been an ideal man on the bench. As a matter of fact he has been a bitter disappointment, not because of any one decision but because of his general attitude."[26]

The close vote in the *Northern Securities* case reflected the difficulty that the judges encountered in trying to distinguish, where the Sherman Antitrust Act appeared to make no distinctions. The problem lay in finding the difference "between combinations whose main purpose was to restrict competition, and those that restricted competiton only incidentally to the main purpose of achieving efficiency in produc- tion."[27] Seven years after *Northern Securities,* the Court announced a new standard that would hereafter be applied to antitrust cases—the "rule of reason." The case involved the Standard Oil Company—no stranger to federal courts. In 1911, Chief Justice Edward White spoke for a unanimous court in holding that Standard Oil had violated the Sherman Act. Much of the opinion, however, was given over to explaining how the Court had arrived at this finding—through applying the "rule of reason."

White proposed that from now on "every contract in restraint of trade" would be interpreted to mean every contract that unreasonably (or unduly) restrained trade. He argued that because the statute used

[24] Letwin, *Law and Economic Policy,* p. 234.
[25] William H. Harbaugh, *Power and Responsibility* (1961), p. 162.
[26] *Letters of Theodore Roosevelt,* ed. Elting Morison (1951), vol. 5, p. 396.
[27] Letwin, *Law and Economic Policy,* p. 252.

general words, leaving definitions to others (which, as we have seen, appears to have been the deliberate intention of the framers), unless judges were free to use some reasonable discretion, then "either they must condemn all actions that could conceivably be called in restraint of trade, or they could not be allowed to condemn any."[28] White insisted that he did not intend to use the rule of reason as an excuse for judicial activism. On the contrary, he appeared to see no incompatibility between his "new" rule and the judicial function of simply enforcing the statute. Of course, any student familiar with the judicial process knows that discretion is inevitably part of it. What White may have been looking for was a doctrine that would make it easier for the Court to resolve future antitrust cases. The rule of reason permitted the Court to accept "the obvious factor that some or many combinations took place innocently, being aimed not at all at monopoly control—and coming nowhere near it—but aimed merely at achieving an economically efficient scale of production."[29] It represented a way to resolve what Holmes objected to in his *Northern Securities* dissent, the possible conflict between statutory language and the actual results intended by the legislation.

Although Justice Harlan agreed that Standard Oil had violated the Sherman Act, he dissented bitterly from the Court's adoption of the rule of reason (see Documents, pp. 159–161).

The White position and Harlan's dissent together reflect the ambivalence that has always been apparent in antitrust policy—how to provide an ordered atmosphere conducive to economic growth and expansion while allowing the maximum individual creative input into this process. This ambivalence had not been resolved by 1915 and indeed may be incapable of solution. American public policy seems to have accepted both standards—large-scale corporate enterprise and antitrust activity—with little awareness of any inherent inconsistency.

[28] Ibid., p. 260.
[29] Ibid., p. 265.

Law and the Lawyer: The Transformation of Legal Education and the Legal Profession

Thus far, this essay has focused on traditional sources of legal history, such as constitutional amendments, statutes, regulatory policy, and cases. However, it would be a serious error to confine analysis to them alone. During the late nineteenth century, the study of law itself was transformed. In 1860 there were approximately twenty-two law schools in the United States. Within thirty years the number had doubled, and by 1910 it had doubled again. In 1880 there were approximately 64,000 lawyers. By 1910 the number totaled over 122,000.[1] In a thirty-year period, the American legal profession has almost doubled. But more had changed than mere numbers. The law school curriculum and the method of instruction were also affected.

Lawyers have always been important in American history. Tocqueville identified them as "the most powerful, if not the only, counterpoise to the democratic element." When Americans became "intoxicated by passion or carried away by the impetuosity of their ideas," they would be checked by the "almost invisible influence of their legal counselors." Lawyers, Tocqueville concluded, "secretly oppose their aristocratic propensities to the nation's democratic instincts, their superstitious attachment to what is old to its love of novelty, their narrow views to its immense designs, and their habitual procrastination to its ardent impatience."[2] In a society rapidly expanding, without a monarchy or

---

[1] Robert Stevens, "Two Cheers for 1870: The American Law School," *Perspectives in American History*, 5 (1971), 428–429, 466; Jerold S. Auerbach, *Unequal Justice: Lawyers and Social Change in Modern America* (1976), p. 94.
[2] Quoted in Stevens, *Unequal Justice*, p. 416.

inherited aristocracy, a landed class, or an influential clergy, it is not surprising that law and lawyers became key elements in social control. They functioned as an "aristocratic meritocracy" and as "technicians of change."[3]

Given the economic growth of the late nineteenth century, replete with its vast corporations, trusts, and holding companies, lawyers became even more dominant in a society they already dominated. By the end of the nineteenth century, as is true today, there were more lawyers in the United States than in any other country in the world. Then, as now, Americans saw legal study leading to power, prestige, and profits. Then, as now, they regarded lawyers from an ambivalent perspective of veneration, envy, respect, and contempt. Then, as now, lawyers seemed absolutely indispensable to American society. Given the present-day obsession with admission to law schools, it might come as a surprise when one examines legal education in the late nineteenth century and notes how easy it was to become a lawyer.

I

The experience of Harvard Law School was not untypical. Before 1870, there appear to have been only two conditions for admission to Harvard Law School: being male and possessing good "moral character." A college degree was not required or even considered necessary. Indeed, by 1829 students not qualified for admission to Harvard College were admitted to Harvard Law School![4] Nor were there any examination requirements—either for admission or for graduation. The length of time needed to complete one's legal studies was eighteen months, or three terms. Any person who had been enrolled for that period of time at Harvard Law School was entitled to a degree "without having necessarily attended a lecture or passed an examination."[5] Frequently, the degree was awarded after the student had left the law school. In 1870 it seemed to be, according to Harvard's new president, Charles W. Eliot, merely "a certificate of residence, with such promise of legal attainments as the responsiveness of the individual to the enthusiasm of his instructors might afford."[6] Finally, it should be noted that in most states

[3] Ibid., pp. 421, 423.
[4] Ibid., p. 418.
[5] Harvard University, *Report of the President 1875–1876*, p. 29; *Green Bag*, 1 (1889), 6.
[6] Charles Warren, *History of the Harvard Law School* (1908), vol. 2 p. 364.

a law degree was not a prerequisite for admission to the bar and thus to the practice of law. Given today's rigorous admission standards and strong competition for entry, one looks back on pre-1870 standards with astonishment and some envy.

In retrospect, however, those standards do not seem unreasonable. The profession and practice of law in America had long predated American law schools. Training for law, in other words, had been almost exclusively "clinical." One did not "go to law school." Rather, one "read law" as an apprentice under the tutelage of another established attorney, who in turn would possibly serve as a sort of sponsor for admittance to the local bar. Such a system had produced some very able lawyers—as, for example, John Adams, Chancellor Kent, Lemuel Shaw, Abraham Lincoln, Daniel Webster, Robert Rantoul, or William Henry Seward—none of whom graduated from, if indeed ever attended, an established law school. Also, some argued that there was an inherent "mystique" to the law, which made it a subject ill suited for classroom teaching. It was better learned by private reading under the supervision of a practicing attorney. Above all, the system seemed to work—if on a somewhat limited, elitist scale.

By the end of the Civil War period, with the establishment of land grant colleges and new state universities, conditions changed: it was now possible for many more to attain a college education. In 1868 the University of Iowa established a law school, as had a private institution, Washington University in St. Louis, one year before. Between 1860 and 1880 numerous law schools were founded, many but not all of them as parts of larger universities. The growing interest in law was reflected not only by increased enrollments but also through acceptance of the idea that, like other bodies of knowledge, law was a subject that could be taught in a university setting, with a professor lecturing and students taking notes, with little or no class discussion. Indeed, until 1870 such was the method widely used at Harvard Law School. Taken together with the very easy terms of admission noted above, it seems the school failed to consider, let alone accept, the need for basic change. At this point, Charles W. Eliot became president of Harvard, and Christopher Columbus Langdell became the first dean of Harvard Law School. Langdell retired as dean in 1895, Eliot as president in 1909. When they passed from the scene, Harvard Law School, along with American legal education in general, had been transformed almost beyond recognition.

Eliot had been an assistant professor of mathematics and chemistry at Harvard but was denied promotion at the end of a five-year appointment. A few years later, in 1865, he was named professor of chemistry at M.I.T. In 1869, Eliot published a two-part article in the *Atlantic Monthly* calling for dramatic changes in the methods and quality of American higher education and noting the "supreme difficulty" in achieving its restructuring—finding qualified leadership. The building up of a new school "must be in the main the work of a single man ... To find this man ... will certainly be the hardest [step] in the whole undertaking." He also criticized the usual American practice of naming clergymen to head colleges and universities. "As a class, ministers are as fit to be suddenly transferred to the bench ... as they are to be put at the head of large educational establishments," he declared. In consequence, Eliot noted, higher education was subject "to such indignity as soldiers feel when untried civilians are put over their heads."[7] A few months after the articles appeared, Harvard elected Eliot as its president. (One can only wonder if the timing was coincidental or not.) The Board of Overseers of Harvard at first rejected the appointment but later approved it, although by a divided vote. Eliot would remain in that post for the next forty years. He had been in office less than one year when he persuaded an again reluctant Board of Overseers to appoint Christopher Columbus Langdell professor of law.

Langdell and Eliot shared a common characteristic in that neither had had the background usually associated with their new positions. Eliot was not a minister nor had he had major exposure to university administration. Traditionally, Harvard professors of law had come to that calling after an eminently successful, if not lengthy, career in law. Langdell had had neither. He had attended Harvard Law School, leaving in 1854. Although highly respected by the few lawyers with whom he had been associated, he was relatively unknown and had had very little actual court practice. In January 1870, Langdell became Dane professor of law at Harvard, and in September he was elected the first dean of the law school, an office he retained for twenty-five years.

II

The Langdell reforms may be divided into three areas: school requirements, faculty, and course content. Langdell had scarcely assumed the deanship when his faculty extended the time required for a law degree

[7] Charles W. Eliot, "The New Education," *Atlantic Monthly*, 23 (1869), pp. 203–220, 358–367. See in particular pp. 365–366.

from eighteen months to two years. At his urging, the school instituted in 1872 a requirement of satisfactory performance or first-year examinations as a condition for continuation into the second year. Although male students possessing "good moral character" and a B.A. degree were almost automatically admitted to Harvard Law School, students without a college degree after 1872 had to take a two-part examination. It consisted of translation at sight from selected Latin classics, although French could be substituted, and questions based on Blackstone's *Commentaries* (see Documents, pp. 162–163). Four years later, the faculty again extended the law degree course of study, to three years. An individual who had been at Harvard Law School for two years, however, could still pass the third year without going to class. By 1899 this option no longer existed, and three years in residence plus satisfactory performance on annual examinations each year were now required of all candidates. Although admission standards remained lax, these reforms tended to make the curriculum more difficult for students once they had been admitted to the law school. Nevertheless, it still remained relatively easy—especially if one had a college degree—to attend Harvard Law School.[8]

Harvard Law School, like other institutions, had continued to select its professors from among well-established and distinguished lawyers. In his annual report for 1871–1872, President Eliot hinted that he was not satisfied with this practice. All the other Harvard faculties, he wrote, "contain a considerable proportion of young men fresh from their studies, possessed of the most recent methods of instruction, and penetrated with the spirit of their generation." The challenge for the law school was to discover what functions "can be well performed by young men who can bring to their work scholarship, zeal, acumen, and a knowledge of their contemporaries, but not much personal experience in the practice of the profession."[9] In his report two years later, Eliot again acknowledged the services of some law teachers "who, though engaged in practice, were willing to lay before the students, in a systematic way, some of the condensed results of their own study and experience." Nevertheless, he insisted, as he had done in 1870–1871 (see Documents, pp. 163–165), that the law school had to rely primarily on

[8] This author well remembers his father's description of being admitted to Harvard Law School in 1923: "I took my diploma, went across to the law school office and registered for classes. That was all."
[9] Harvard University, *Report of the President 1871–72*, p. 23.

"resident professors, who make teaching their business, and the welfare of the school their chief concern."[10]

As if to suit the action to the words, Langdell and Eliot in June 1873 persuaded an extremely reluctant Harvard Board of Overseers to appoint James Barr Ames as an assistant professor of law. Only twenty-seven years old, Ames had not practiced law at all! Indeed, he had never left Harvard Law School, having received his law degree in 1872 and remained there for an additional year of study. Looking back in 1895 at this "radical" experiment, Eliot noted correctly that Harvard Law School "had never done it; no school had ever done it; it was an absolutely new departure in our country in the teaching of law."[11] Ames attained distinction both as a legal scholar and as a teacher. He succeeded Langdell as dean in 1895, and his career at Harvard Law School lasted for more than thirty-five years.

The choice between appointing young scholar-teachers with no experience in practice as against selecting seasoned veterans of the law remains controversial to this day: many law schools have attempted to strike some sort of balance between the two "extremes." Eliot and Langdell faced much opposition to their actions. In his report for 1881–1882, the Harvard president again discussed the rationale behind the new departure. Harvard law professors "must be men who possess large and systematic knowledge of law, sound judgment, enthusiasm, and the power of clear exposition." They did not need to be, however, "eminent at the bar or on the bench." Indeed, rarely had "the same man achieved eminence both in practice and as a teacher." Eliot insisted that "the teaching of law is a difficult and honorable profession in itself, and cannot be combined with, or late in life taken up in exchange for, the practice of law, another absorbing profession which appeals to different motives, develops different qualities, and holds out different rewards." He cited an alternative method of recruitment: that of selecting "young men of mark" with a genius for law and "a desire for the life of a teacher." After being "carefully tested on probationary appointments," such individuals should be "made professors at an age so early that the whole vigor of their youth and prime could be thrown into teaching and authorship." But here, perhaps, Eliot demonstrated some presidential caution. After admitting that Harvard had followed this pattern with Ames, and that the university might "try the method again," he added "without, however, adopting it as a policy."[12]

[10] Harvard University, *Report of the President 1873–74*, p. 26.
[11] Warren, *Harvard Law School*, p. 389.
[12] Harvard University, *Report of the President 1881–1882*, pp. 31–32.

By 1886, Dean Langdell no longer felt it necessary to demonstrate any caution at all on this subject. He informed the Harvard Law School Association that "what qualifies a person...to teach law is not experience in the work of a lawyer's office, not experience in dealing with men, not experience in the trial or argument of causes—not experience in short, in using law, but experience in learning law."[13] Langdell's emphasis on learning law reflected a basic assumption, shared by President Eliot, that law was a science, a self-contained body of knowledge with its own postulates and principles. Other conclusions then logically followed. If law be a science, argued Langdell, "it will scarcely be disputed that it is one of the ... most difficult of sciences, and that it needs all the light that the most enlightened seat of learning can throw upon it."[14] Hence the study of law properly belonged only in a university, *not* in a law firm.

Further, the scientific method involved observation and analysis of specific phenomena from which general principles could be derived. These principles, presumably, could then be used to test the validity of future specific observations. Langdell argued that for a law student, the "specimens" and specifics were judicial opinions, which were to be examined with microscopic care. Like a scientist, a law student had to learn the skills of careful scrutiny and "discriminating classification."[15] Applied to the law, such skills would enable the student to grasp the fundamentals of cases, extracting the principles and applying them to other legal issues, or knowing when and why they should not be so applied.

As with virtually all of Langdell's convictions and proposals, his belief that law was a science received President Eliot's strong support. Indeed, during Langdell's first year at Harvard, Eliot had written that "law is emphatically a science, with a method and a history; it has a language of its own."[16] Himself a scientist, Eliot later described the appointment of James Barr Ames as an attempt to see "if it were practicable to breed professors of law by the same gradual process by which competent teachers are trained up in other departments of the university. This interesting experiment has thus far been perfectly successful."[17]

---

[13] Warren, *Harvard Law School*, p. 361.
[14] Arthur E. Sutherland, *The Law at Harvard* (1967), p. 175.
[15] Ibid., p. 176.
[16] Harvard University, *Report of the President 1870–1871*, p. 17.
[17] Harvard University, *Report of the President 1873–1874*, p. 27.

It would be a mistake to carry Langdell's analogy between the study of law and laboratory observations too far. Nor did he. Physical laws (e.g., gravity) do not change, whereas the American polity alters its law with great regularity. However, as Arthur Sutherland has stated, Langdell's "insistence on scrupulously exact examination of legal materials, on their classification according to essential likenesses and differences, were disciplines of great value." This method "provided admirable material for such training in the hard-eyed scrutiny of any writing, in perception of the relevant and rejection of the irrevelant, in logical progression from premise to conclusion." Students trained "in such intellectual processes could use them in any phase of legal study."[18]

For Langdell, the most important result of his law-as-a-science thesis was the introduction of the *case method* of teaching law. It meant an end to the traditional lecture approach, whereby a student passively took notes as the professor lectured. Langdell insisted that each student have his own collection of cases in front of him during the class. Putting the "scientific method" to work required, "first careful study of the material, then discussion with others, submission to questioning, justification of the student's judgment, or [admission] of error when error became apparent."[19] The student would thus be better able to "classify the cases, to distinguish like from unlike despite superficial similarity, to reject as useless opinions which were ill-reasoned, based on bad logic, and hence were flawed specimens, unsuitable for generalization." Underlying Langdell's case method were two assumptions. The first was "that principles were best discovered in appellate court opinions"; hence "clinical or practical experience had nothing to add to the education of the lawyer."[20] Moreover, politics, economics, social theory, and other subjects were also unnecessary for legal education. Indeed, they were a waste of a law student's valuable time.

The second assumption was that intensive analysis of selected appellate opinions would correct "the judicial deviations from established principles" that Langdell believed had "occurred in preceding decades."[21] Here again, he emphasized the ability to apply and reapply these basic principles "with constant facility and certainty to the ever-tangled skein of human affairs." An extremely conservative doctrine, this emphasis on judicial scientism was in reality a sophisticated

---

[18] Sutherland, *Law at Harvard*, p. 178.
[19] Ibid., p. 177.
[20] Stevens, *The American Law School*, p. 437.
[21] Ibid.

endorsement of judicial supremacy. Indeed, judges lay at the heart of Langdell's case system. A theoretical common law on the national level would virtually control all the state courts.[22]

Although rejected and disparaged at first, Langdell's case method ultimately won acceptance at every major American law school. To this day, it remains an extremely important tool in the process of legal education. Popularly known as the "Socratic method," this technique was most recently reflected in the movie and television series *The Paper Chase*. To be sure, its very serious weaknesses are more apparent today than one hundred years ago. There is much more to law than cases and judicial opinions. Indeed, contemporary legal education gives great attention to administrative and statutory issues as well as to private law. Further, it is obvious today as it may not have been in 1880 that law is a very complex field of study; it is not possible to base a sound legal education on a few basic principles.

Nevertheless, between 1880 and 1915 Langdell's case method was virtually unchallenged. Writing of Langdell's accomplishments twenty years after he became dean, Eliot noted that this period had been "full of fundamental changes, serious risks, grave criticisms, and severe anxieties; but the changes have proved wise, the risks have been run without disaster, the criticisms have been met or outgrown, and the anxieties have been forgotten in the crowning success."[23] Grant Gilmore has noted that this "great age of the American law school has long since passed and will never come again." It may be, he adds, that "no educational institutions in any country at any time have enjoyed the prestige and achieved the success" of the law schools that matured in "the image of Langdell's Harvard." To graduate from one of those schools "was a guaranty of success. To be a professor of law on one of the great faculties was to hold a passport to fame and fortune."[24]

It may be a little unfair to describe Langdell as "an essentially stupid man who, early in his life, hit on one great idea to which, thereafter, he clung with all the tenacity of genius."[25] Important results flowed from his innovations, not all of them positive. In the first place, legal education at the select, prestigious schools became very elitist. It is difficult to reconcile the Langdell law school and its staff of full-time professors, not practitioners, with the image of a democratic bar—its

[22] Joel Seligman, *The High Citadel: The Influence of Harvard Law School* (1978), p. 36.
[23] Harvard University, *Report of the President 1888–1889*, p. 21.
[24] Grant Gilmore, *The Ages of American Law* (1977), p. 57.
[25] Ibid., p. 42.

Lincoln types studying by candlelight, learning law by themselves. Further, the rise of the full-time, university-oriented law schools affected the part-time night schools. These institutions charged lower fees, used part-time instructors, and made legal education available to many urban students with full-time jobs. For many immigrant families, or individuals from a "different" background such as eastern European, black, Jewish, or Italian, they offered the only opportunities to a legal career. "Between 1890 and 1910 the number of day schools [full-time] increased from 51 to 79 or 60 percent, while the number of night schools [part-time] soared from 10 to 45, or 350 percent."[26] Even today, a stigma of second-class quality still attaches in general to night law school legal education—in many instances reflecting an unjustified prejudice lingering from an earlier age.

III

The tensions between the full-time and part-time law schools reflected the obvious but important fact that by the late nineteenth century, lawyers were in great demand. The legal profession itself had become "one of America's growth industries."[27] Its expansion accompanied that of technological, corporate, and industrial elements so much in evidence. The Langdell case method as well as the appearance of such professional legal associations as the American Bar Association or the Bar Association of the City of New York reflected the complexities of the new era.[28] The concept of *what* a lawyer did, and *how* it was to be done underwent dramatic transformation.

Before Langdell came to Harvard Law School, principles of law rather than precedents of decisions were emphasized. These principles were expounded in law schools usually by distinguished attorneys, whose "teaching texts" were in fact their own experiences as trial lawyers. The advent of readily available, and increasingly complete, reports and digests on both the state and federal levels was indispensable for Langdell's new technique of teaching. The law student no longer heard about the cases, he had to read them himself. He no longer had the principles taught to him in lectures; he had to isolate them himself through intensive discussion and Socratic dialogue. With the number of

---

[26] Auerbach, *Unequal Justice*, p. 95.
[27] Harold C. Livesay, *Samuel Gompers and Organized Labor in America* (1978), p. 137.
[28] George Martin, *Causes and Conflicts* (1970).

printed volumes ever expanding, precedents became more and more important. As one lawyer wrote, "on the whole, the effect of the large number of adjudged cases contained in the reports has virtually transformed the profession from a class of lawyers able to practice without law books, to a class almost entirely dependent on the adjudged cases."[29]

One result of this change was the need for large law libraries, something that the small firms of an earlier day could not afford. One of the chief purposes behind the new professional bar associations was to provide its members with the reference tools now needed for legal practice. Another was to mitigate the growing impersonality that seems always to accompany expansion. Increasingly, large law firms resulted in a loss of that sense of collegiality that once had seemed so important. A bar association provided a place for lawyers to meet, talk, and compare notes. Moreover, an association of lawyers would be able to have some input into the problem of professional standards and quality—a source of some tension, especially since the numbers, both of prospective lawyers and of law schools, had increased so much. The bar association could serve, also, as a sort of watchdog over the actions of established lawyers. In this respect, the efforts of the newly founded Bar Association of New York City to break up the "infamous" Tweed Ring, replete with its own lawyers and judges, are of interest.[30] An active bar association might serve to restore the somewhat jaded image of the attorney in late-nineteenth-century America.

---

[29] Ibid., p. 196. See also pp. 193, 197.

[30] The exact amount of money "stolen" from New York City by the Tweed Ring will never be known. In April 1871, one of the new Bar Association's founders concluded that the cost of governing the city "had risen from $36,000,000 in 1868 to $136,000,000 in 1870." But it was not clear "where the money had gone." George Martin compares the estimated value of items in the "Tweed Courthouse" with the actual expense:

	Value	Cost
Safes	$ 3,450	$ 482,500
Carpets	19,000	4,829,426
Furniture	309,000	1,849,400
Plumbing	74,000	1,114,875
Plastering	70,000	2,870,464
Carpentry	30,000	2,189,700
	$505,450	$13,336,365

As an example of how the stealing was done, Tweed is said to have replied to a contractor who offered to put in an electric fire alarm system for $60,000, "if we get you a contract for $450,000, will you give us $225,000?" Ibid., pp. 61, 63.

The era of the great trial lawyers seemed over. Now lawyers were seen less in the court room and more in corporate board rooms. They stayed in the background, arranging "deals" for their clients. They counseled their clients not only on what they should or should not do, but on what steps to take if they got caught. And as the Tweed Ring era so well indicates, sometimes lawyers were as corrupt as their clients (see Documents, pp. 165–170).

The Langdell era and the accompanying emergence of professional bar associations raised difficult questions regarding both the purposes of legal study and the future of the profession. Should legal education train practitioners, or should it make law into a responsive social institution?[31] Should the practice of law be open to all who qualified, or should it be a career for the selected best? These issues were divisive and troubling in 1915; they remain so today. One did not and does not like to admit that professional advancement and success in law are dramatically affected by "race, religion, class, color, sex, education, educational opportunity, and social origins—rather than hard work, self-discipline, inductive reasoning skills and academic achievement."[32] Of course such differentials existed long before Langdell's deanship, but his changes, together with the major shifts in American society between 1870 and 1900, made them more obvious. By emphasizing law as a science, by "detaching process from purpose," lawyers in the Langdell mold could avoid nagging questions of political and social import and at the same time claim that law was "an avenue for service, not a means for private gain."[33]

Similarly, law professors could insist on the need to prepare lawyers for roles of service to the community, while at the same time training them for employment in a large corporate law firm. If young lawyers chose to enter private corporate practice, and few outstanding graduates from the best schools did not, it was in part because they had been so well prepared for their jobs in law school. As the United States entered World War I, the tensions caused by the emergence of a stratified bar had not been resolved. The influence of a predominantly white Protestant legal elite has been long lasting. "If you seek its monument, look around."

---

[31] Auerbach, *Unequal Justice,* p. 95.
[32] Ibid., p. 4.
[33] Ibid., p. 154.

Law, Judges, and Social Change: The Gospel According to President and Ex-President Theodore Roosevelt

There is a tendency to see law as impersonal, and elements of legal history—statutes, cases, and opinions—as dull and irrelevant. Although understandable, this tendency should not be carried too far. One must note a human dimension to law. Primarily it affects and is affected by people. Popular perception of a society's legal system may be a valuable tool in assessing its effectiveness. One political figure whose personality was anything but dull, and whose career between 1900 and 1912 was of great public relevance, sensed the continuing importance of legal institutions for American society. He well understood the tensions between the desired role and the actual rule of law, with its underlying strength and ambivalence.

Historical evidence of this ambivalence is not lacking. Americans flaunted their devotion to English legal tradition, yet at the same time used mobs to destroy property and intimidate persons during the Stamp Act crisis that preceded the Revolution. By the 1830s, the Bill of Rights in the Constitution had been held applicable to the federal government, yet federal authorities in the Southern states, to say nothing of congressional leadership, systematically prevented discussion and dissemination of antislavery petitions and writings. The nation glorified constitutionalism, yet by the 1850s some lawyers were urging the existence of a higher law that justified disobedience to constitution and statute. American society has had more lawyers than any other, yet their presence has not prevented numerous lynchings over the years, especially in the South. The vaunted American obsession with "due process" has been matched by an impatient desire—sometimes verging

55

on the ruthless—to get things done and to set forces in motion toward the accomplishment of economic and industrial goals.

========================= I =========================

Theodore Roosevelt's "preparation" for the presidency was unusual if not unique. His previous careers included training for the law at Columbia University Law School, election as a New York State legislator, and being a Dakota cowboy, president of a Western stockmen's association, United States civil service commissioner, police commissioner of New York City, assistant secretary of the United States Navy, a ranking officer of the most famous volunteer regiment to serve in the "splendid little war" (the Spanish-American War of 1898), governor of New York, and Vice-President of the United States. Yet there was more. Fluent in several languages, habitually reading anywhere from one to three books a day, Roosevelt also possessed a remarkably urbane mind. Before he turned forty-three, he had written multivolume histories of the American West and the War of 1812, several biographies, and some fourteen additional volumes of history, literary criticism, natural history (TR was a "skilled ornithologist, paleontologist, and taxidermist"), and political philosophy, and about seventy-five thousand letters.[1]

And all this, as his most recent (and best) biographer Edmund Morris emphasizes, took place *before* TR became the youngest president in American history. By the time of his death in 1919, ten years after he left the White House, his total of books stood at thirty-eight, his letters numbered about 150,000, and he had experienced several additional careers.[2] Indeed, Roosevelt was more than the possessor of the broadest intellect ever to occupy the presidency. With the possible exception of his cousin Franklin, he was also the nation's most popular President.

Given this amazing range of accomplishments linked to a mercurial personality and occasionally brash behavior (though rarely unintentionally so), TR both inspired and authored numerous expressions of strong feeling. In 1898, on the eve of the Spanish-American War, the impatient TR (then assistant secretary of the Navy) allegedly called his

[1] Edmund Morris, "Theodore Roosevelt, President," *American Heritage* 32 (June–July 1981), 7.
[2] Ibid.

boss, President McKinley, "a white-livered cur," one with "no more backbone than a chocolate eclair."[3] He apparently referred to Charles Evans Hughes (the only person to serve on the United States Supreme Court for two separate periods) as "a psalm-singing son of a bitch."[4] During the "diplomatic" activity that helped to produce the Panama Canal, TR described various South American political figures as "a corrupt pithecoid community," "inefficient bandits," "foolish and homicidal corruptionists," and "contemptible little creatures."[5] Perhaps the most famous example—add one that reflects his deep ambivalence between proper procedure and the desire for tangible results—was his statement about the Panama Canal. "If I had followed traditional, conservative methods I would have submitted a dignified state paper of probably 200 pages to Congress and the debates on it would have been going on yet; but I took the Canal Zone and let Congress debate; and while the debate goes on, the Canal does also."[6]

Inevitably, TR was on the receiving end as well. Henry Adams (the perennial pessimist and brother of the Charles Francis Adams mentioned in an earlier chapter) noted that Roosevelt was "pure act."[7] A not too friendly British critic concluded that TR's Oxford lecture on "Biological Analogies in History" was mostly "Longitude, Latitude and Platitude."[8] Another English observer nominated him as one of the world's leading "masters of the obvious."[9] Mark Twain complained that TR "dug so many tunnels under the Constitution that the transportation facilities enjoyed by that document are rivalled only by the City of New York."[10] A famous member of the House of Representatives who for some years exercised almost dictatorial control over that establishment claimed: "Roosevelt's got no more respect for the Constitution than a tomcat has for a marriage license."[11] Even those working closely with

---

[3] Thomas A. Bailey, *A Diplomatic History of the American People* (1940), p. 506.

[4] Morris, *Roosevelt*, p. 6.

[5] Bailey, *Diplomatic History*, pp. 538-539.

[6] Ibid., p. 545. Recent research has cast some doubt on whether in fact TR actually used the words "took the canal." However, he never retracted them, and they remain an excellent example of his impatience with lengthy legal procedures. See James F. Vivian, "The 'Taking' of the Panama Canal Zone: Myth and Reality," *Diplomatic History* 4 (1980): 95-100. I am much indebted to my colleague Professor Warren Kimball for calling the Vivian article to my attention.

[7] George Mowry, *The Era of Theodore Roosevelt* (1958), 109.

[8] *Letters of Theodore Roosevelt*, ed. Elting Morison (1954), vol. 7, p. 650.

[9] Mowry, *Roosevelt*, p. 109.

[10] Morris, *Roosevelt*, p. 14.

[11] Ibid.

TR as members of his cabinet were sometimes unable to resist the temptation to take a jab at their chief. "Ah, Mr. President," said one such member on hearing a Roosevelt proposal. "Why have such a beautiful action marred by any taint of legality?"[12]

II

TR's career, especially after he became President in 1901, is of interest for this study because of his persistent emphasis on the responsiveness of law to needed change, especially in the context of the modern American industrial system. Not himself a lawyer (he never completed Columbia Law School), Roosevelt knew better than many attorneys the important relationship between law and change. Not only was it increasingly necessary for, as he put it, "the common elements" to get justice. "It is even more important that they should be made to feel and see that they are getting it."[13] The legal process should promote not impede this development. Given his astute insight into an area that caused great tension during his lifetime, one wonders why TR had abandoned his study of law at a relatively early age.

It is probably an exaggeration to conclude that the young Roosevelt "aligned the moral law and the common law and was shocked at the discrepancy."[14] But TR did write later of his brief experience as a law student at Columbia University that "some of the teaching of law books and of the classroom seemed to me to be against justice." Looking back on this period, he observed in 1913: "I was young; there was much in the judgment which I then formed . . . which I should now revise; but, then as now, many of the big corporation lawyers, to whom the ordinary members of the bar then as now looked up, held certain standards which were difficult to recognize as compatible with the idealism I suppose every high-minded young man is apt to feel."[15] Roosevelt's idealism was tempered by a fear of social violence and agitation that remained a part of his political philosophy. He never resolved the ambivalence between this fear and the intense antipathy he felt toward corporate policies and judicial decisions that he believed contributed strongly to the potential for such violence. At first, TR blamed labor unions and "agitators" for social unrest. By 1907, however, he had concluded that judicial attitudes

[12] William Harbaugh, *The Life and Times of Theodore Roosevelt* (1975), p. 177.
[13] *Works of Theodore Roosevelt* (1925), vol. 19, p. 128.
[14] Harbaugh, *Roosevelt,* p. 17.
[15] Theodore Roosevelt, *Autobiography* (1913), p. 61.

and certain resulting decisions represented a much greater threat to American society.

In his reaction both to the Pullman strike of 1894 and to the 1896 presidential campaign, a young Roosevelt echoed the usual Republican conservative viewpoint. Opponents of the injunction as a tool against strikers were "cave dwellers," seeking to force "the country into anarchy." Politicians such as William Jennings Bryan and labor leaders such as Eugene Debs would transform Lincoln's Gettysburg model of government of the people, by the people, and for the people into a government "of a mob, by the demagogue, for the shiftless and the disorderly and the criminal." Indeed, Roosevelt argued, Bryan had built his campaign on "all the ugly force[s] that seethe beneath the social unrest," and his appeal, based on "class and sectional hatred," had received unwarranted support from organized labor.[16] When TR wrote to his close friend Massachusetts senator Henry Cabot Lodge shortly after President McKinley had been shot, he sounded like a thoroughgoing reactionary. "We should war," he said, "with relentless efficiency not only against anarchists, but against all active and passive sympathizers with anarchists." Conveniently forgetting how important the newspaper publisher William Randolph Hearst had been in whipping up popular enthusiasm for war with Spain, TR now denounced him. "Every scoundrel like Hearst and his satellites who for whatever purpose appeals to and inflames evil human passion, has made himself accessory...to every crime of this nature, and every soft fool who extends a maudlin sympathy to criminals has done likewise."[17]

======   III   ======

During his first message to Congress, delivered on December 3, 1901, Roosevelt hinted that his views concerning capital, labor, and links with government had changed. Like no other President before him, TR acknowledged that Americans held a "widespread conviction" that the trusts "are in certain of their features and tendencies hurtful to the general welfare." Such conviction, he believed, was based on the assumption "that combination and concentration should be, not prohibited, but supervised and within reasonable limits controlled; and

[16] Howard Hurwitz, *Theodore Roosevelt and Labor in New York State, 1880–1900* (1943), pp. 179, 181, 185.
[17] *Letters*, vol. 3, p. 142.

in my judgement this conviction is right."[18] Roosevelt went much further in his observations about the American worker. Emphasizing that he referred only to federal employment, the new President called for enforcement of the eight-hour day. "Excessive hours of labor," as well as "all night-work for women and children" should be prohibited.[19] Having offered the expected tribute to the traditional emphasis on the individual's own qualities and abilities, TR promptly added: "Second only to this comes the power of acting in combination or association with others." Great good, he concluded, "has been and will be accomplished by associations or unions of wage-workers," especially "when they combine insistence upon their own rights with law-abiding respect for the rights of others."[20]

A year later, the President reiterated these views in even stronger language. The government, he insisted, was not "attacking the corporations, but endeavoring to do away with any evil in them." This was not hostility but a determination "that they shall be so handled as to subserve the public good. We draw the line against misconduct, not against wealth."[21] Unlike many of his Republican colleagues, Roosevelt consistently equated large unions with large corporations. "This is an era of federation and combination." Just as modern business works through corporations and "it is a constant tendency of these corporations to grow larger, so it is often necessary for laboring men to work in federations." Such unions "have become important factors of modern industrial life."[22] Corporations and unions alike were capable of much good and much evil. Thus "opposition to each kind of organization should take the form of opposition to whatever is bad in the conduct of any given corporation or union—not of attacks upon corporations as such nor upon unions as such."[23]

TR's comments in 1902 came in the wake of his unique role in settling a coal strike, one that had caused the greatest work stoppage thus far in American industrial development. Although conditions in the mine fields were acknowledged to be awful, the mine operators refused to make any compromises whatsoever. Miners "don't suffer," claimed the owners' chief spokesman, George Baer. "Why, they can't

[18] *Works,* vol. 17, p. 104.
[19] Ibid., p. 108.
[20] Ibid., p. 109.
[21] Ibid., p. 164.
[22] Ibid., p. 171.
[23] Ibid., p. 172.

even speak English."[24] Although it seems difficult to believe, Baer actually topped the stupidity of this remark. As the strike dragged on, he proclaimed that miners would be protected and cared for "not by the labor agitators, but by the Christian men to whom God in his infinite wisdom has given the control of the property interests of the country."[25]

The 1902 coal strike was ultimately settled by a presidential commission—the first time that national authority had been used to resolve rather than break a strike. Unlike the situation in 1894, Roosevelt blamed the operators and not the strikers for the long work stoppage. He had sought, he later recalled, to save these "big propertied men . . . from the dreadful punishment which their own folly would have brought on them." The operators were "so blinded" that they could not understand that the President "was trying to save them from themselves and to avert . . . the excesses which would have been indulged in at their expense if they had longer persisted in their conduct." The operators failed to comprehend that their property rights "were of the same texture as were the human rights, which they so blindly and hotly denied." But the interests of both the miners and the operators had to be subordinated to "the fundamental permanent interests of the whole community."[26]

While Roosevelt remained insistent about the need for effective federal corporate regulation and the necessity to distinguish between "good" trusts and "bad," by 1906 he was troubled about the relations between organized labor and the courts. Like other perceptive observers, TR was well aware that between 1890 and 1912 "there was in fact a developing conflict in our society at least as dangerous to the country's welfare as the conflict that rattled the nation from 1840 to 1860."[27] At issue was the process by which Americans were trying to "satisfy their needs as human beings," as they confronted the awesome industrial power that was now an inextricable part of their lives. How, in short, was it possible "to order, successfully, an industrial society?"[28] Here, Roosevelt believed that the courts could play an important role, especially by acting as a sort of buffer between labor and capital. Always a severe critic of labor violence, the President became even more critical of capitalistic intransigence that appeared to make violence an attractive

---

[24] Harbaugh, *Roosevelt*, p. 169.
[25] Ibid., p. 173.
[26] *Autobiography*, pp. 510, 512–513.
[27] *Letters*, vol. 3, p. xiv.
[28] Ibid., p. xv.

if not inevitable alternative. Judges, he insisted, especially because of the role they had come to play in resolving disputes, should be very sensitive and even-handed in dealing with labor and capital.

In his message for 1906, the President insisted that there "must be no hesitation in dealing with disorder." But likewise the injunction power should not be abused, "as is implied in forbidding laboring men to strive for their own betterment in peaceful and lawful ways." Nor should it be used "merely to aid some big corporation in carrying out schemes for its own aggrandizement."[29] Roosevelt was even more harsh in his private correspondence. "I do not at all like the social conditions at present," he wrote to William Howard Taft in 1906. In particular, the President noted "the dull, purblind folly of the very rich men; their greed and arrogance, and the way in which they have unduly prospered by the help of the ablest lawyers, and too often through the weakness or shortsightedness of the judges."[30]

By 1907, TR was admitting that there was "warrant" for some of the attacks levied against the injunction. "Where it is [used] recklessly or unnecessarily, the abuse should be censured, above all by the very men who are properly anxious to prevent any effort to shear the courts of this necessary power."[31] Roosevelt also strongly endorsed the concept of workmen's compensation, although he again limited his endorsement to "all positions, public and private, over which the National Government has jurisdiction."[32] He suggested that payment by the employer for accidents should "be automatic instead of being a matter for lawsuits. Workmen should receive certain and definite compensation for all accidents in industry irrespective of negligence."[33] The benefits of the law were obvious to the President, although not perhaps to lawyers who made their living from litigating such cases. "Employers would gain a desirable certainty of obligation and get rid of litigation to determine it, while the workman and his family would be relived from a crushing load."[34] As will be seen shortly, TR considered workmen's compensation an important tool to cope with the harsh realities of industrial life; and the fact that the doctrine ran counter to a popular legal philosophy made no difference at all to him.

[29] *Works,* vol. 17, p. 407.
[30] *Letters* vol. 5, p. 183.
[31] *Works,* vol. 17, p. 507.
[32] Ibid., p. 508.
[33] Ibid., p. 509.
[34] Ibid.

In 1908, his last full year as President, TR so deepened the gap between himself and the main body of Republican conservatives as to make it virtually unbridgeable. Forming the vast majority of the Republican party, these men had supported Roosevelt unwillingly while distrusting him unwaveringly. TR sent a special message to the Republican-controlled Congress in January 1908, insisting that judges had sometimes used the injunctive power "heedlessly and unjustly"—inflicting on occasion "irreparable wrong upon those enjoined." Now Roosevelt bluntly warned his party that if some way was not found to stop these judicial abuses, "the feeling of indignation against them among large numbers of our citizens will grow so extreme as to produce a revolt against the whole use of the process of injunction."[35] As the Republican members of Congress listened in silence, the message went on to criticize judges who failed in their duty to the public by improper dealings with lawbreaking corporations and lawbreaking men of wealth. Proposing that 10,000 extra copies of the message be printed, one representative noted that "it was the best Democratic doctrine I have ever heard emanating from a Republican source."[36]

By December 1908, Roosevelt had become a lame duck President, his successor already elected and much of his party restive under his unrelenting suggestions for change. Roosevelt's last annual message was typical: he categorized the reactionary as "the worst enemy of order" and noted pointedly that "the men who defend the rights of property have most to fear from the wrongdoers of great wealth." He repeated once again his conviction that "a blind and ignorant resistance to every effort for the reform of abuses and for the readjustment of society to modern industrial conditions represents not true conservatism, but an incitement to the wildest radicalism; for wise radicalism and wise conservatism go hand in hand."[37] Not surprisingly, TR turned again to the subject of judges. "In no other nation in the world do the courts wield such vast and far-reaching power as in the United States." Yet, "we must face the fact that there are wise and unwise judges." It was even more important, then, that "the duty of respectful and truthful criticism, which should be binding when we speak of anybody, should be especially binding when we speak of them." Judges, insisted the outgoing President should "do justice and work equity, so that they may

---

[35] 42 *Cong. Record,* Part 2 (1908), 1347–1363.
[36] Ibid., p. 1363.
[37] *Works,* vol. 17, pp. 580, 587.

all persons in their rights, and yet break down the barriers of privilege, which is the foe of right."[38]

<h1 style="text-align:center">IV</h1>

For more than a year after he left the White House, TR traveled abroad, visiting heads of state and hunting big game in Africa. (I trust, noted one of his critics, that some lion will do its duty.) For reasons beyond the scope of this study, Roosevelt's successor, William Howard Taft, managed to deepen the split between conservatives and insurgents within the Republican party. Far away, Roosevelt watched and worried. In April 1910, he wrote to Henry Cabot Lodge of his fears that "the right type of aggressive leadership" was lacking in Washington, because it was the type of leadership that "a lawyers' Administration is totally unfit to give." Indeed, he added, "there is not a greater delusion than the belief that a lawyer is, *per se,* also a statesman."[39] In another letter to Lodge one month later, TR warned that "unless we are content to face disaster to the judiciary in the future, there must be a very radical change in the attitude of our judges to public questions.... The conduct of the bench in failing to move with the times, and in continually sticking on minor points of the law rather than turning to broad principles of justice and equity, is one of the chief elements in producing the present popular discontent."[40]

Not content with writing his views to his correspondents, the former President began to "go public." In August 1910, he spoke to a joint session of the Colorado legislature, and noted that the courts had not recognized new conditions but rather had lagged behind, thus creating a sphere in which neither state nor nation had effective control, "and where the great business interests that can call to their aid the ability of the greatest corporation lawyers escape all control whatsoever."[41] Roosevelt gave as an example the famous 1905 Supreme Court decision in *Lochner v. New York,* wherein the justices had invalidated a New York statute that set maximum hours bakery employees could work.[42] Regarding this decision TR exclaimed:

[38] Ibid., pp. 607, 606.
[39] *Letters,* vol. 7, p. 74.
[40] Ibid., p. 80.
[41] *Outlook,* 96 (1910), 149.
[42] *Lochner v. New York,* 198 U.S. 45 (1905).

By a five-to four vote they declared the [statute] unconstitutional, because, forsooth, men must not be deprived of their "liberty" to work under unhealthy conditions. All who are acquainted with the effort to remedy industrial abuses know the type of mind which may be perfectly honest, but is absolutely fossilized, which declines to allow us to work for the betterment of conditions among the wage-earners on the ground that we must not interfere with the "liberty" of a girl to work under conditions which jeopardize life and limb, or the "liberty" of a man to work under conditions which ruin his health after a limited number of years.

Expanding on his remarks for publication in September 1910, TR insisted that they were not "an attack upon the judiciary as a whole, an incitement to riot, and an appeal to the passions of the mob."[43]

Late in 1910, during the campaign for the congressional elections, TR returned to the "attack" against the judiciary. He specifically criticized the chief justice of the Connecticut Supreme Court, Simeon Baldwin, a dull but distinguished jurist. In a well-known case dealing with workmen's compensation, Baldwin had declared the federal statute involved unconstitutional. Acceptance today of workmen's compensation as a fundamental part of American industrialism should not obscure the fact that in the early twentieth century the doctrine was highly controversial. Why should this be so?

As late as the 1890s and thereafter, the legacy of American individualism still remained attractive, even as the assembly line together with the realities of urban-industrial life made it increasingly anachronistic. A legal doctrine that reflected this legacy was "freedom of contract," a late-nineteenth-century variation on the theme of substantive due process discussed in Chapter 1.[44] *Lochner v. New York,* the bakery working hours case so sharply criticized by TR, is a classic example of the doctrine. According to the majority, it was none of the state's business how many hours mature bakery workers could spend on the job; it was a matter solely between the two parties to a contract, the bakery owner and his employees.

In the workmen's compensation statute, Congress sought to place definite responsibility on the railroads for various accidents to their employees. To ensure that the corporations would be bound to this obligation, the statute added that "any contract ... the purpose or intent

---

[43] *Outlook,* 96 (1910), 150.
[44] On "freedom of contract," see Charles C. Goetsch, *Essays on Simeon Baldwin* (1981), pp. 87–92, 112–116, including the sources cited in his notes.

of which shall be to enable any common carrier to exempt itself from any liability created by this act, shall to that extent be void."[45] In other words, even if both parties wanted to do so, they *could not* make an agreement relieving the railroad of its liability. It was this provision that Chief Justice Baldwin held unconstitutional, ruling that it tended "to deprive the parties to such a contract of liberty and property without due process of law."

TR criticized Baldwin's opinion so severely that the chief justice threatened to sue the former President for libel. Roosevelt accused Baldwin of being perfectly willing to enforce the contractual rights of railroad workers to give up their benefits, even if they lost life or limb in the process. "The right to contract to get killed is property of which they cannot be deprived."[46] For Roosevelt, the case was dramatic evidence of the unresponsiveness of judges to needed change. When Baldwin wrote to TR requesting a retraction of certain comments, Roosevelt not only refused but, in replying to Baldwin, made his criticism and his reasons for it even more explicit.

I criticized your decision because it is to me an incredible perversion of the Constitution of the United States. I criticized it because it is not only reactionary but revolutionary, I criticized it because I am against Socialism, and this decision and every decision like it makes for Socialism, or something worse. Every strained construction of the Constitution which declares that the nation is powerless to remedy industrial conditions which cry for law gives aid to these enemies of our American system of government who wish to furnish in its place some new, vague and foolish substitute.[47]

Unhappy with this reply, Baldwin persisted, publicly hinting that a libel suit would be forthcoming. Roosevelt's further response to the judge who had, incidentally, just been elected governor of Connecticut, gave little satisfaction. TR assured Baldwin that "I was actuated by no feeling of personal rancor or hostility." On the other hand, "I feel too deeply on the principle involved in this controversy . . . to avoid the issue in such a suit."[48] Again, he detailed for Baldwin why he found the opinion so offensive. His comments were typical of the man; emphatic yet perceptive, self-righteous yet astute in comprehension of what American industrialism had actually come to mean.

[45] *Letters*, vol. 7, p. 150.
[46] Ibid.
[47] Ibid.
[48] *Outlook*, 97 (1911), 241.

The so-called freedom of contract which you have enunciated in that decision is a relic of barbarism. It is an empty and imaginary theory of freedom which is opposed to the known fact that to a large extent there is no freedom in the contract which the employee makes with the great employer. He has to take in countless instances his employment under such rules as the employer may impose, and if the employer may impose by a rule or a "contract" the denial of rights created by a statute, intended to operate in the employee's favor, the theory of the employee's freedom in accepting that rule or making that contract is a delusion and a sham. The theory of "freedom," of which you are the resolute defender in this opinion, would, if extended, undermine the very basis of all the child labor legislation in the United States, and of all legislation regulating industry to prevent the exploitation of human lives where excessive competition threatens them, and where long hours and evil conditions of labor are destructive of manhood and womanhood. It would undermine every law intended to make living conditions more tolerable for working people. If the workman has a right to contract to take the risk of being killed through the negligence of his employer, has a right to contract to receive no benefit from a statute which is created to afford him a benefit, he has a right to contract to live in a filthy tenement, and laws requiring property-owners to make these tenements habitable can be undermined and nullified as limiting the "freedom" of the tenement dweller to live in filth and pestilence. And yet you think that this issue between legal barbarism and the enlightened judgment of all humane and right-thinking men is so petty and personal that it can be settled by a slander or libel suit brought by you against me.

Your decision against the Federal Employment Liability Act can in my view be justified only by adhering to an economic philosophy of government which I hold would result in making and keeping the workman in a state of helplessness so far as his own rights are concerned. The lawmaker branches of our State and National Governments are recognizing the necessity of making these changes, so as to better the position of the workman, crippled in industry and in his fight for redress and justice in the courts. Your decision in a very fundamental matter denies not merely justice to the workman, but lies like a dead tree in the very pathway of remedial justice by declaring powerless the branch of government from which this redress must come.[49]

Shortly after receiving TR's letter, Baldwin replied, informing him that there would be no libel suit. Possibly occupied with his new career as governor of Connecticut, probably aware that given TR's popular reputation, a guilty verdict would be very unlikely—whatever the reasons, Baldwin was now willing to let the controversy die.

[49] Ibid., p. 243.

Although Roosevelt showed no hesitation or self-doubt in responding to Baldwin, he realized that much of the editorial comment concerning the threatened lawsuit was very critical of himself, not the chief justice. TR admitted this fact when he wrote to Henry Cabot Lodge that the "great body of lawyers and businessmen who have come to the conclusion that the judges are the bulwarks of property against the people, have been bound to misrepresent everything I said where a judge was concerned."[50] In fact, there was more involved in the entire incident than either Baldwin or Roosevelt clearly articulated.

Baldwin's decision, one that relied heavily on liberty of contract, was characteristic of a type of jurisprudence variously labeled as "legal formalism," "classical legal thought," or "mechanical jurisprudence." It assumed that there were a series of fundamental and unchangeable legal principles that, in theory at least, made the judicial function relatively simple. All the judge had to do as to apply the appropriate principle. It was, supposedly, a *totally objective* process that had nothing to do with a judge's own social, philosophic, or economic predilections. Much in vogue during the late nineteenth century, classical legal thought came under heavy attack from those critics, such as TR, who well understood the great potential that personal values play in judicial decisions. Moreover, these critics resented what Charles Goetsch has called "the real social harm" caused by such decisions.[51] The workmen's compensation litigation was typical, in that it severely hampered the ways in which American society could respond to the pressures of industrialization. Baldwin and TR represented more than two sides of a disagreement. Each typified an approach toward judicial action that ultimately was irreconcilable. Although it would not become clear until a generation after TR's death, the heyday of classical legal thought had passed.[52]

V

Even as the threat of a lawsuit evaporated, TR expanded his critique of the courts. Slowly, between 1911 and 1912, he developed a plan to deal with immovable judges and "impossible" decisions. Early in 1911, Roosevelt published a series of articles on the judiciary. By January

[50] *Letters,* vol. 7, p. 217.
[51] Goetsch, *Baldwin,* p. 92.
[52] But see Robert G. McCloskey, "Economic Due Process and the Supreme Court: An Exhumation and Reburial," *1962 Supreme Court Review,* p. 34.

1912, when his major piece, "Judges and Progress," appeared, the goal of his proposal was clear, as were some of the troubling implications behind it. Although, as will be seen, TR was unable to resolve the problem of judicial decisions and popular rule, the fact that he spent so much time and energy on it indicates his great concern.

As he had done with Baldwin, Roosevelt disclaimed any personal criticism of judges, focusing rather on those jurists "cursed with an obsession for... mechanical jurisprudence. The stickler for technicalities, the man who treats precedents, however outrageous, as always binding... will often do as much harm" as those judges who "reflect special sympathy or antipathy towards a certain class of his fellowmen."[53] He enthusiastically quoted the Supreme Court of Oklahoma: "We confess to a want of respect for precedents which were found in the rubbish heap of Noah's Ark, and which have outlived their usefulness, if they ever had any."[54] Possibly with his controversy concerning Baldwin still fresh in his mind, Roosevelt insisted that "no person should by contract be permitted to impose substantial restraints upon his liberty. Freedom to impose [them], if given to weak and needy people, simply amounts to defeating the very end of freedom."[55] The article from which these excerpts have been taken appeared in the *Outlook* for March 11, 1911. In his piece for the next issue, Roosevelt began to get down to specifics.

Never hesitant to quote those legal scholars or even judges who agreed with him, and some did, TR cited the famous article by Roscoe Pound (later to become professor and dean at Harvard Law School) about liberty of contract[56]—a work on which TR drew heavily in his critique of the *Lochner* case. He claimed that courts were ultimately "the servants of the people and responsible to the people." How could this fact be balanced with the equally obvious need for judicial independence? If one opposed short terms for elected judges as well as some method of judicial recall, and TR insisted that he did, what was the alternative? It was "that there shall be full and free and effective criticism of the court whenever [it] acts on some great question of policy and principle, as to which the people have a right to decide, and where their decision, and not that of their servants must ultimately stand." Those who "make up a decisive and permanent majority of the State or

[53] *Outlook,* 97 (1911), 533.
[54] Ibid., p. 534.
[55] Ibid., pp. 534–536.
[56] Roscoe Pound, "Liberty of Contract," *Yale Law Journal,* 18 (1909), 457.

Nation ... have a right to try the experiment," whether it be in the area of workmen's compensation or limiting the hours of work in a bakery.[57] Indeed, "when a great question of policy arises, and when ... as the evident expression of permanent popular will, the people have determined what a given policy is, it should be carried into effect." TR concluded with reiteration of one of his favorite arguments. "The men who denounce ... free and fair criticism of the judiciary ... are themselves doing all in their power to render necessary the adoption of some more direct method of popular control."[58]

Even as these articles appeared, the New York State Court of Appeals handed down a decision declaring that state's workmen's compensation statute unconstitutional. An unsigned editorial in the *Outlook* for April 8, 1911, pointed out the anomalous state of affairs. "The extraordinary result is that a law which the employers want, which the employees want, which the Legislature wants, which the people in general want, which, in brief, everyone wants except a few employers, certain accident insurance companies, and a class of not highly esteemed lawyers who prosecute accident suits for a share of the damages recovered, cannot be had by a democratic community."[59] Roosevelt had his turn in the issue of May 13, where he denounced the court, and proposed a more specific remedy than that which he had outlined earlier—although he still could not be specific as to how his proposal would be implemented.

Again insisting on the "very high regard" in which he held the judiciary, the former President added that "ours is a democracy, and we the people have the right to rule when we have thought out our problems and come to a definite decision."[60] This applied to judges as well. The people should "think coolly," and "come to a well-settled conclusion before they can act against a judge. But they must have the power to act." Moreover, this authority should apply when the people have decided that "any judge, no matter how upright and well-intentioned, is fundamentally out of sympathy with a righteous popular movement, so that his presence on the bench has become a bar to orderly progress for the right." TR then turned to the New York State Court of Appeals. Its decision represented not interpretation of the law but rather "the

[57] *Outlook,* 97 (1911), 576.
[58] Ibid., p. 577.
[59] Ibid., p. 752.
[60] *Outlook,* 98 (1911), 52.

enactment of judge-made law in defiance of legislative [action]." It was not only judge-made law but made "in a way oppressive, well nigh ruinous to the interests of the wage workers, and indeed to society as a whole. It is out of the question that the courts should be permitted permanently to shackle our hands as they shackle them by such decisions as this.... Such decisions are profoundly anti-social, are against the interests of humanity, and tell for the degradation of a very large portion of our community; and above all, they seek to establish as an immutable principle the doctrine that the rights of property are supreme over the rights of humanity."[61]

Roosevelt, perhaps thinking of himself and the unpleasant decision he would soon have to make about running again for the presidency in 1912, noted the lesson of history. It "teaches us that when people become goaded to action by a long course of abuses they are apt to reject the leadership of moderate reformers, and to go to violent extremes, in the effort to provide a remedy."[62] Even worse than the court's decision was what it implied; "such contemptible futility" in our government "from the standpoint of remedying wrong and injustice." Sounding yet again an increasingly favorite refrain, TR concluded that "the so-called conservatives who work for and applaud such decisions, and deprecate criticism of them, are doing all in their power to make it necessary for the Nation as a whole in these matters to go to a far more radical extreme."[63]

In his private correspondence during 1911, Roosevelt was even more candid. "If I could really get the people aroused here," he wrote concerning the Workmen's Compensation case, "I should try to take every man off the bench who made that decision, upon the ground that a judge capable of making it was unfit to be trusted with the delicate complex and highly responsible duty of the court in the presence of our struggle for better things, socially and industrially."[64] It was one thing, and inappropriate at that, to enlarge national power arbitrarily through

---

[61] Ibid., pp. 53–54.
[62] Not all observers were impressed with TR's frequent tendency to attack special interests and at the same time mount an equally drastic assault on reformers who wanted to go too far. Robert LaFollette, a senator from Wisconsin with whom TR tangled bitterly during the 1912 campaign, wrote of Roosevelt: "In this way he sought to win approval, both from the radicals and the conservatives. This cannonading, first in one direction and then in another, filled the air with noise and smoke, which confused and obscured the line of action, but, when the battle cloud drifted by and quiet was restored, it was always a matter of surprise that so little had been accomplished." Robert M. LaFollette, *Autobiography* (1913), p. 479.
[63] *Outlook*, 98 (1911), 54.
[64] *Letters*, vol. 7, p. 291.

judicial construction. But it was even worse for the judiciary to "arbitrarily diminish the power by refusing to understand and apply the old principles under the new conditions."[65] TR wished "in some fashion," that "the people should be allowed to express their judgment on any construction of the Constitution by the judges, and this expression should be final."[66] Yet, he did not "wish a snap judgement of the people to be taken." It was not that "our judges are corrupt, but they are absolutely reactionary, and their decisions...have been such as almost to bar the path to industrial, economic and social reform. By such decisions they add immensely to the strength of the Socialist Party, they perpetuate misery, they increase unrest and discontent."[67]

Between late 1911 and the middle of 1912, TR finally conceptualized as clearly as he could his proposal for "correcting" judicial decisions. The January 1912 article, "Judges and Progress," appears at first glance to be a rehash of much that he had already written privately and publicly. Actually, he went much further. After citing a string of cases similar to the New York Workmen's Compensation decision, TR claimed that these decisions reflected judicial devotion "not to the Constitution, but to a system of social and economic philosophy which...is not only outworn, but to the last degree mischievous, because of its utter unsuitability to existing social and economic conditions." He insisted moreover that "if a majority of the people after due deliberation decide to champion such social and economic reforms as those we champion, they have the right to see them enacted into law and become a part of our settled governmental policy."[68] This could be done by giving the voters "the right if they so desire, in any given case, to vote finally as to whether or not the [judicial] decision is to be accepted as binding." Debate should not be hasty; thus the vote "should not be taken within, say, six months of the decision."[69] I do believe, Roosevelt concluded, "that this people must ultimately control its own destinies, and cannot surrender the right of ultimate control to a judge any more than to a legislator or an executive." Possibly as an afterthought, he added three short sentences. "What I have advocated is not revolution. It is not wild radicalism. It is the highest and wisest kind of conservatism."[70]

[65] Ibid., p. 319.
[66] Ibid., p. 424.
[67] Ibid., p. 421.
[68] *Outlook*, 100 (1912), 43.
[69] Ibid., p. 46.
[70] Ibid., p. 48.

One of the truly great American jurists who corresponded with Roosevelt about his idea was Learned Hand, although in 1911–1912, Hand's outstanding reputation was still largely in the future. While Hand agreed with Roosevelt's criticism of many decisions, he did not like the basic implication behind the plan. In reality, TR proposed a way of putting popular pressure on judges in advance, seeking thereby to ensure certain outcomes in key cases. Hand believed this type of approach to be "either impracticable, or, as I think, very dangerous." Furthermore, Hand might well have asked if judges could function properly in an atmosphere with something like a sword of censure hanging over their heads, ready to be activated by popular agitation.

TR replied to Hand's letter: "I absolutely agree with you as to bringing pressure to bear on the judges, but in Constitutional cases, the alternatives must be to have the right of appeal from the judges." In these cases, "the people shall have the right to vote as to whether or not the judges' interpretation of the law in such a case is correct, and . . . their vote shall be decisive."[71] As he wrote to another correspondent in June 1912, "all I propose to do in a certain number of cases, where a court declares an act of the legislature . . . unconstitutional, then after due deliberation to let the people themselves decide whether the court or the legislature is to be sustained." He did not "propose to make the legislature supreme over the court; I propose merely to allow the people, after ample deliberation, to decide whether they will follow the legislature or the court."[72] His plan "was not to recall judges who gave wrong constitutional decisions, but to recall the decisions" themselves.[73]

By limiting his plan to certain constitutional cases, and to judicial decisions not individual judges, TR acknowledged the great stature enjoyed by the courts in America. Even so, noted a contemporary, Robert Grant, the distinction between changing a constitutional doctrine by amendment, as opposed to Roosevelt's plan for "popular votes on specific cases . . . is a little vague, and has served incidentally to throw the property-owning class and all reverers of our institutions into pink fits."[74]

As the former President expanded his quest for the 1912 Republican presidential nomination from inaction to frenetic effort, his discussion of courts and judges merged into a broader political platform known as

[71] *Letters,* vol. 7, p. 441.
[72] Ibid., p. 553.
[73] Ibid., p. 652.
[74] *Letters,* vol. 8, pp. 1459–1460.

the New Nationalism. TR claimed that "we are the true conservatives, for in the long run it will be found that the only true conservative is the man who resolutely sets his face toward the future, and strives to give wise guidance to those who are struggling towards the idea of fairer dealings between man and man."[75] Insisting that he was a layman not a lawyer, TR nevertheless here described the classic function of the attorney in American legal history. After he and his supporters had bolted the Republican convention to form the Bull Moose progressive party, Roosevelt wrote to a close friend that "wise progressivism and wise conservatism go hand in hand, and . . . the wise conservative must be a progressive because otherwise he works only for that species of reaction which inevitably in the end produces an explosion."[76] Arguing that somehow our legal order had forgotten these axioms, TR's writings as discussed here represented a unique challenge to bring law and change into better balance. That his particular solution may not have been feasible in no way diminishes the credit due to him for undertaking to raise these questions in the first place.

Summary

Although Colorado did enact a statute calling for a type of "judicial decision recall," TR did not succeed in his efforts to have such a procedure widely adopted.[77] A generation later, his cousin Franklin Roosevelt also failed in his attempt to alter the composition of the United States Supreme Court. Both Roosevelts had objected to judges blocking legislation that they and duly elected representatives of the people obviously desired. Popular opinion, although critical of judicial obstructionism, apparently did not extend to tampering with the system. On the other hand, both Presidents while losing the battle may have won the war. Their campaigns concerning judicial responsibility and accountability made the justices more aware of their peculiarly antidemocratic function in a democratic polity. Judges, it has been observed, do follow the election returns; and the causes that had aroused both Presidents ultimately were sustained by the courts. TR wrote in 1911: "[As President] I tried, and I now continue to try to teach lessons

[75] *Letters*, vol. 7, p. 514.
[76] Ibid., p. 597.
[77] Ibid., p. 650.

that I feel ought to be learned by my fellow countrymen, and I often wonder how much I am accomplishing by it. There are so many important lessons that ought to be learned."[78] In 1913, when he published his own account of what can only be called a remarkable career, it was with the knowledge that his days as a prominent political power were ended. He reaffirmed yet again his insistence that "our worst revolutionaries today are those reactionaries who do not see and will not admit that there is need for change."[79] In 1910 he had written to Henry Cabot Lodge, "I care nothing whatever for popularity, excepting as a means to an end. Of course I like to have the good will and respect of those for whom I care, but wide popular acclaim, it seems to me, counts for almost nothing unless it can be turned to good tangible account, in the way of getting substantial advance along the lines of clean and wise government.... I want to accomplish things."[80]

When the United States entered the World War, a conflict that TR would not live to see finally resolved, the American legal system had not yet gained the proper balance between law and change. In his lifetime, the industrial, social, geographic, and economic contours of American society had been transformed. One vital function of any legal system, especially the American one, is that it lessens the shock of change by somehow cushioning it in a context of continuity while at the same time providing for innovative adaptation to the new and the changing. As the era of Theodore Roosevelt ended, it was unclear to what extent the American legal framework had fulfilled this function. More than half a century later, it still may well be an unanswered question.

QUESTIONS

1.   The issue of judicial accountability has long troubled thoughtful Americans. Why should a judge be accountable to the public in the first place?

2.   Should judges be elected or appointed? Is the issue of accountability better resolved if they are appointed? If they are elected?

3.   Why would conservatives be upset at TR's proposal? How does it differ from the traditional process of amending a state constitution?

4.   How much judicial independence is compatible with public accountability?

[78] Ibid., p. 331.
[79] Roosevelt, *Autobiography*, p. 525.
[80] *Letters*, vol. 7, p. 81.

Documents

I.

Civil Rights Enactments 1865–1868

The Thirteenth Amendment (1865)

Section 1. Neither slavery nor involuntary servitude, except as a punishment for crime whereof the party shall have been duly convicted, shall exist within the United States, or any place subject to their jurisdiction.

Section 2. Congress shall have power to enforce this article by appropriate legislation.

QUESTIONS

1. In terms of the words used in the amendment, is it broad or narrow in its coverage?

2. Note the exception clause in section 1. Why, do you think, was it included?

3. Given the fact that by the time of the Thirteenth Amendment's ratification, American slavery (largely because of the presence of the Union armies in the South) was virtually nonexistent, why was the amendment deemed necessary?

4. Judging from the wording, is there a justification for concluding that the amendment was intended to apply to more than slavery as it had existed prior to 1865?

The Civil Rights Act of 1866*

An act to protect all Persons in the United States in their Civil Rights, and furnish the Means of their Vindication.

Be it enacted by the Senate and House of Representatives of the United States of America in Congress assembled, That all persons born in the United States and not subject to any foreign power, excluding Indians not taxed, are hereby declared to be citizens of the United States; and such citizens, of every race, color, without regard to any

---

* *Statutes of the United States,* 39th Cong.,/1st Sess. (1866), Chapter 31, p. 27-28.

previous condition of slavery or involuntary servitude, except as a punishment for crime whereof the party shall have been duly convicted, shall have the same right, in every State and Territory in the United States, to make and enforce contracts, to sue, be parties, and give evidence, to inherit, purchase, lease, sell, hold, and convey real and personal property, and to full and equal benefit of all laws and proceedings for the security of person and property, as is enjoyed by white citizens, and shall be subject to like punishment, pains, and penalties, and to none other, any law, statute, ordinance, regulation, or custom, to the contrary notwithstanding.

Sec. 2. And be it further enacted, That any person who, under color of any law, statute, ordinance, regulation, or custom, shall subject, or cause to be subjected, any inhabitant of any State or Territory to the deprivation of any right secured or protected by this act, or to different punishment, pains, or penalties on account of such person having at any time been held in a condition of slavery or involuntary servitude, except as a punishment for crime whereof the party shall have been duly convicted, or by reason of his color or race, than is prescribed for the punishment of white persons, shall be deemed guilty of a misdemeanor, and, on conviction, shall be punished by fine not exceeding one thousand dollars, or imprisonment not exceeding one year, or both, in the diescretion of the court.

Sec. 3. And be it further enacted, That the district courts of the United States, within their respective districts, shall have, exclusively of the courts of the several States, cognizance of all crimes and offences committed against the provision of this act, and also, concurrently with the circuit courts of the United States, of all causes, civil and criminal, affecting persons who are denied or cannot enforce in the courts or judicial tribunals of the State or locality where they may be any of the rights secured to them by the first section of this act; and if any suit or prosecution, civil or criminal, has been or shall be commenced in any State court, against any such person, for any cause, whatsoever, or against any officer, civil or military, or other persons, for any arrest or imprisonment, trespasses, or wrongs done or committed by virtue or under color of authority derived from this act or the act establishing a Bureau for the relief of Freedmen and Refugees, and all acts amendatory thereof, or for refusing to do any act upon the ground that it would be inconsistent with this act, such defendant shall have the right to remove such cause for trial to the proper district or circuit court in the manner prescribed by the "Act relating to habeas corpus and regulating judicial proceedings in certain cases," approved March three, eighteen hundred and sixty-three, and all acts amendatory thereof.

QUESTIONS

1. Note that this is the first federal statute ever to define American citizenship. Why, do you think, was a definition not deemed necessary until 1866?

2. Although the act is supposed to protect persons "in their civil rights," does it define these rights?

3. What rights are supposedly protected by the statute, and would they be called civil rights today? Would what we commonly call civil rights be protected by this statute today?

4. Does the third section of the statute provide any insights into the changing relationship between the states and the federal government after 1865?

The Fourteenth Amendment (1868)

Section 1. All persons born or naturalized in the United States, and subject to the jurisdiction thereof, are citizens of the United States and of the State wherein they reside. No State shall make or enforce any law which shall bridge the privileges or immunities of citizens of the United States; nor shall any State deprive any person of life, liberty, or property, without due process of law; nor deny to any person within its jurisdiction the equal protection of the laws.

Section 2. Representatives shall be apportioned among the several States according to their respective numbers, counting the whole number of persons in each State, excluding Indians not taxed. But when the right to vote at any election for the choice of electors for President and Vice President of the United States, Representatives in Congress, the executive and judicial offices of a State, or the members of the legislature thereof, is denied to any of the male inhabitants of such State, being twenty-one years of age, and citizens of the United States, or in any way abridged, except for participation in rebellion, or other crime, the basis of representation therein shall be reduced in the proportion which the number of such male citizens shall bear to the whole number of male citizens twenty-one years of age in such State.

• • •

Section 5. The Congress shall have power to enforce, by appropriate legislation, the provisions of this article.

QUESTIONS

1.   Note the wording of section 1. Is it narrow or broad in scope? What specific evidence from the actual words in the section supports your answer? Do the words provide any clues as to the "intentions" of the framers?

2.   What does section 2 actually mean? It has, as far as this author has been able to establish, *never* been put into effect. Why do you think this has been the case?

3.   What are the implications of section 5 for future use of the amendment?

4.   Which section(s) of the amendment do you consider to be most important? Why?

5.   What are some of the similarities and differences between the Thirteenth Amendment, the Fourteenth Amendment, and the Civil Rights Act of 1866?

II
Southern Statutes 1865–1866

The Southern states, faced with an end to slavery, perceived an absolute necessity for statutes that would define if not regulate the behavior and status of the freedmen. The four statutes excerpted here were typical of such laws.

*Mississippi Vagrant Law (1865)**

Sec. 1. That all rogues and vagabonds, idle and dissipated persons, beggars, jugglers, or persons practicing unlawful games or plays, runaways, common drunkards, common night-walkers, pilferers, lewd, wanton, or lascivious persons, in speech or behavior, common railers

*Walter L. Fleming, *A Documentary History of Reconstruction,* vol. 1 (1906), pp. 283–285.

and brawlers, persons who neglect their calling or employment, misspend what they earn, or do not provide for the support of themselves of their families, or dependents, and all other idle and disorderly persons, including all who neglect all lawful business, habitually misspend their time by frequenting houses of illfame, gaming houses, or tippling shops, shall be deemed and considered vagrants, under the provisions of this act, and upon conviction thereof shall be fined not exceeding one hundred dollars, with all accruing costs, and be imprisoned, at the discretion of the court, not exceeding ten days.

Sec. 2. All freedmen, free negroes and mulattoes in this State, over the age of eighteen years, found on the second Monday in January, 1866, or thereafter, with no lawful employment or business, or found unlawfully assembling themselves together, either in the day or night time, and all white persons so assembling themselves with freedmen, free negroes or mulattoes, or usually associating with freedmen, free negroes or mulattoes, on terms of equality, or living in adultery or fornication with a freed woman, free negro or mulatto, shall be deemed vagrants, and on conviction thereof shall be fined in a sum not exceeding, in the case of a freedman, free negro, or mulatto, fifty dollars, and a white man two hundred dollars, and imprisoned at the discretion of the court, the free negro not exceeding ten days, and the white man not exceeding six months.

Sec. 3. All justices of the peace, mayors, and alderman of incorporated towns and cities of the several counties in this State shall have jurisdiction to try all questions of vagrancy in their respective towns, counties and cities, and it is hereby made their duty, whenever they shall ascertain that any person or persons in their respective towns, counties, and cities are violating any of the provisions of this act, to have said party or parties arrested, and brought before them, and immediately investigate said charge, and, on conviction, punish said party or parties, as provided for herein. And it is hereby made the duty of all sheriffs, constables, town constables, and all such like officers, and city marshals, to report to some officer having jurisdiction all violations of any of the provisions of this act, and it shall be the duty of the county courts to enquire if any officers have neglected any of the duties required by this act, and in case any officer shall fail or neglect any duty herein it shall be the duty of the county court to fine said officer, upon conviction, not exceeding one hundred dollars, to be paid into the county treasury for county purposes....

Mississippi Statute re Certain Offenses of Freedmen (1865)*

Sec. 1. That no freedman, free negro or mulatto, not in the military service of the United States government, and not licensed so to do by the board of police of his or her county, shall keep or carry fire-arms of any kind, or any ammunition, dirk or bowie knife, and on conviction thereof in the county court shall be punished by fine, not exceeding ten dollars, and pay the costs of such proceedings, and all such arms or ammunition shall be forfeited to the informer; and it shall be the duty of every civil and military officer to arrest any freedman, free negro, or mulatto found with any such arms or ammunition, and cause him or her to be committed to trial in default of bail.

Sec. 2. Any freedman, free negro, or mulatto committing riots, routs, affrays, trespasses, malicious mischief, cruel treatment to animals, seditious speeches, insulting gestures, language, or acts, or assaults on any person, disturbance of the peace, exercising the function of a minister of the Gospel without a license from some regularly organized church, vending spirituous or intoxicating liquors, or committing any other misdemeanor, the punishment of which is not specifically provided for by law, shall, upon conviction thereof in the county court, be fined not less than ten dollars, and not more than one hundred dollars, and may be imprisoned at the discretion of the court, not exceeding thirty days.

Sec. 3. If any white person shall sell, lend, or give to any freedman, free negro, or mulatto any fire-arms, dirk or bowie knife, or ammunition, or any spirituous or intoxicating liquors, such person or persons so offending, upon conviction thereof in the county court of his or her county, shall be fined not exceeding fifty dollars, and may be imprisoned, at the discretion of the court, not exceeding thirty days....

Sec. 5. If any freedman, free negro, or mulatto, convicted of any of the misdemeanors provided against in this act, shall fail or refuse for the space of five days, after conviction, to pay the fine and costs imposed, such person shall be hired out by the sheriff or other officer, at public outcry, to any white person who will pay said fine and all costs, and take said convict for the shortest time.

---

* Fleming, pp. 209–210.

North Carolina Black Code (1866)*

Sec. 2. . . . All persons of color who are now inhabitants of this State shall be entitled to the same privileges, and are subject to the same burthens and disabilities, as by the laws of the State were conferred on, or were attached to, free persons of color, prior to the ordinance of emancipation, except as the same may be changed by law.

Sec. 3. Persons of color shall be entitled to all the privileges of white persons in the mode of prosecuting, defending, continuing, removing and transferring their suits at law and in equity; and likewise to the same mode of trial by jury, and all the privileges appertaining thereto. And in all proceedings in equity by or against them, their answer shall have the same force and effect in all respects as the answer of white persons. . . .

Sec. 9. Persons of color not otherwise incompetent shall be capable of bearing evidence in all controversies at law and in equity, where the rights of persons or property of persons of color shall be put in issue, and would be concluded by the judgment or decree of court; and also in pleas of the State, where the violence, fraud, or injury alleged shall be charged to have been done by or to persons of color. In all other civil and criminal cases such evidence shall be deemed inadmissible, unless by consent of the parties of record: *Provided,* That this section shall not go into effect until jurisdiction in matters relating to freedmen shall be fully committed to the courts of this State: *Provided, further,* That no person shall be deemed incompetent to bear testimony in such cases because of being a party to the record or in interest . . .

Sec. 11. Any person of color convicted by due course of law of an assault with an attempt to commit rape upon the body of a white female, shall suffer death.

Sec. 12. The criminal laws of the State embracing and affecting a white person are hereby extended to persons of color, except where it is otherwise provided in this act, and whenever they shall be convicted of any act made criminal, if committed by a white person, they shall be punished in like manner, except in such cases where other and different punishment may be prescribed or allowed by this act . . . .

* Fleming, pp. 291-293.

South Carolina Vagrancy Statute (1865)*

VAGRANCY AND IDLENESS

XCV. These are public grievances, and must be punished as crimes.

XCVI. All persons who have not some fixed and known place of abode, and some lawful and reputable employment; those who have not some visible and known means of a fair, honest and reputable livelihood; all common prostitutes; those who are found wandering from place to place, vending, bartering or peddling any articles or commodities, without a license from a District Judge, or other proper authorities; all common gamblers; persons who lead idle or disorderly lives, or keep or frequent disorderly or disreputable houses or places; those who, not having sufficient means of support, are able to work and do not work; those who (whether or not they own lands, or are lessees or mechanics,) do not provide a reasonable and proper maintenance for themselves and families; those who are engaged in representing, publicly or privately, for fee or reward, without license, any tragedy, interlude, commedy, farce, play or other similar entertainment, exhbition of the circus, sleight-of-hand, wax works, or the like; those who, for private gain, without license, give any concert or musical entertainment, of any description; fortune-tellers; sturdy beggars; common drunkards; those who hunt game of any description, or fish on the lands of others, or frequent the premises, contrary to the will of the occupants, shall be deemed vagrants, and be liable to the punishment hereinafter described.

XCVII. Upon information, an oath of another, or upon his own knowledge, the District Judge, or a Magistrate, shall issue a warrant for the arrest of any person of color known or believed to be a vagrant, within the meaning of this Act. The Magistrate may proceed to try, with the assistance of five freeholders, or calling to his aid another Magistrate, the two may proceed to try, with the assistance of three freeholders, as is provided by the Act of seventeen hundred and eighty-seven, concerning vagrants; or the Magistrate may commit the accused to be tried before the District Court. On Conviction the defendant shall be liable to imprisonment, and to hard labor, one or both, as shall be fixed by the verdict, not exceeding twelve months.

---

*Fleming, pp. 309-310.

QUESTIONS

1. Compare these statutes with the Civil Rights Act of 1866. Are they inconsistent with its provisions?

2. Note especially the excerpt from the North Carolina Black Code. How is it similar to the Civil Rights Act? How does it differ from that act?

3. Do these statutes provide any indication as to tne future course of race relations in the South later in the nine*teenth century?

III.

Civil Rights Cases Relating to the Fourteenth Amendment 1873-1896

The Slaughter-House Cases:
Lawyers' Briefs *

BRIEF FOR PLAINTIFFS IN ERROR—J. A. CAMPBELL, ATTORNEY

John Campbell, author of the two briefs filed on behalf of the butchers, was a former member of the United States Supreme Court. He resigned his seat when his native state, Alabama, seceded from the Union in 1861.

...There are forty millions of population who may refer to [the Fourteenth] Amendment to determine their rank in the United States, and in any particular State. There are thirty-seven Governments among the States to which it directs commands, and the States that may be hereafter admitted, and the persons hereafter to be born or naturalized will find here declarations of the same weighty import to them all....

All men are to have their rights to life, liberty and property ascertained before deprivation. Each citizen is to have his privileges and immunities undiminished; liberty; the right to personal freedom; the power of determining, by his own choice, his own conduct; to have no master, no overseer put over him; to be able to employ himself without

---

* *Landmark Briefs and Arguments of the Supreme Court of the United States: Constitutional Law,* vol. 6 (1975), pp. 536–586, 639–653, 734–763.

constraint of law or owner; to use his faculties of body and mind, at places and with persons chosen by himself, and on contracts made by himself. All these things grow out of the [Thirteenth and Fourteenth] amendments, and are held under the safeguard of the nation.—These things being secured, all other things would follow. But the amendments secure the more important and the most imperiled of the consequential rights. They protect property. They compel to equal protection.

Thus the social right to combine his faculties with those of others, to profit by the combination; to share in the conquests of the society over nature on equal terms are also secured....

The 14th Amendment embodies all that the statesmanship of the country has ordained for accommodating the Constitution and the institutions of the country, to the vast additions of territory, increase of the population, multiplication of states and territorial governments, the annual influx of aliens, and the mighty changes produced by revolutionary events, and by social, industrial, commercial development....

...That State laws must be so framed as to secure life, liberty, property from arbitrary violation, and protection of law shall be secured to all. Thus as the great personal rights of each and every person were established and guarded, a reasonable confidence that there would be good government, might seem to be justified.

Unquestionably a very large share of blessings are stored and garnered here as in a common repository. Here is the hope of the laboring man; the confidence and trust of the merchant; the stability, success and profit of the agriculturist; the leisure and inspiration of the student, and the peace, the comfort, the enjoyment of the family and the home. Much that governments can afford are comprehended in the proper enforcement of the command of this article....

I have assumed that the 14th Amendment was not adopted as an act of hostility; nor designed to sow discord; nor to answer an ephemeral or unworthy purpose. Those who deprive the first section of its vitality, and demand an interpretation which would leave the State Governments, in possession of their powers over persons and property unimpaired, do place a stigma upon the authors of the Article.... The language of the section to the State Governments to maintain prescribed bounds, and to Congress to enforce obedience to the command, is imperative. The excesses apprehended are invasions of the personal rights of individuals under color of authority.—Two forms of invasion are apprehended. The State may deny individual rights and liberties and claim to perform all of the offices and duties of society, and under the names of socialism, communism, and other specious pretences, control all the revenues and labors of the State. Or the advantages, benefits, partialities and privileges of the State may be conferred upon a few to the detriment and oppression of the people....

The 14th amendment is not confined to any class or race. It comprehends all within the scope of its provisions. The vast number of laborers in mines, manufactories, commerce, as well as the laborers on the plantations are defended against the unequal legislation of the States. Nor is the amendment confined in its application to the laboring man.

The mandate is universal in its application to persons of every class and every condition of persons.

Under the decisions of this court the bulwarks that have been erected around the investments of capital are impregnable against State legislation. The obligation of contracts has been asserted with vigor, and the scope of the provision under the administration of the court is nearly as comprehensive as the dealings of men. Labor under the 14th amendment is placed under the same protection. The signs of the time very plainly show that the protection has not been extended too soon.

...We do not contend that the plaintiffs in this court have been placed in handcuffs and carried to the houses, pens and yards of this corporation, with violence, to labor for this corporation of seventeen as African slaves might have been; nor have they been imprisoned or confined to compel them to labor with these parties. But all of them have been prohibited from doing their usual or customary work, except upon the property and for the compensation and profit of these parties. They have been compelled to close up the houses and other conveniences of business to enable this corporation to construct and use profitably theirs. All men in all places are commanded to forbear doing the acts that would infringe the privileges granted to this corporation. Any obstruction to the enjoyment of these privileges is removed by the strong arm of the State. The common rights of men have been taken away, and have become the sole and exclusive privilege of a single corporation. Can a State Legislature say that religion, speech, publication and invention shall be carried on and employed in designated limits, under the superintendence of the seventeen persons, and in their houses, yards or pens? The same law that protects them protects the personal right to labor. The constitution declares that none of these privileges can be abridged by State laws....

In prohibiting slavery forever, the constitution must have prohibited something actually continuing and pernicious, and ordained in its place something having the same characteristics of reality and duration. The freeman cannot be assimilated to the dead, but is inspired with a perennial hope of improvement, and with the right to labor for that improvement. In prohibiting slavery forever, the fundamental rights of men are declared to be the aim and end of the national existence. Therefore, the first section of the Fourteenth Amendment is a corollary to the thirteenth, as was the Civil Rights Act that preceded it, an echo of it. That amendment and that act instituted and organized freedom in laws, and guaranteed its protection against sordid interests, selfish aims and ambitious usurpations, or greedy appetites. These amendments to the constitution placed the freedom of every American citizen under the protection of a common law. They have established a national government, which is sovereign not merely in the external affairs of the nation, but in regard to life, liberty, property, privilege, immunity, and the right to an equal protection from State governments; and to secure these, it comes in contact with every citizen, and makes itself felt in his dearest and most intimate relations. So closely is the right to work with freedom so closely associated with all other rights, that a political contest affecting that right has created a necessity for a change of the whole constitution of the government in its relations to personal rights and State connections with them. . . .

The abolition of that condition of persons implied in the words "Held to service to labor," has had the effect to set at liberty three millions of persons, to remodel the Constitution of the United States, to establish theoretically a law of equality in civil and political rights, and to repress arbitrary, tyrannical, unjust laws for the abridgement of the natural power and liberty of men to provide for themselves freely, and without tribute to the cupidity or avarice of monopolists, or suborners of depraved legislatures and profligate governors. The question before us is, does it accomplish this end? The act under consideration prohibits industry within three parishes in an important and extensive business to hundreds of persons, unless they will labor at the houses and yards of a single corporation—the laborer to pay at fixed rates for the privilege, and with an inhibition of the erection or the use of any others. . . .

Is it not too much to say that the position of laboring men in the State, and the interests of laboring men in society, at this moment, create a more profound interest than all other questions that come before cabinets, councils or legislative assemblies. The only interest that the civil war that has profoundly affected this country will permanently excite, is what solution did it make of the questions that arise and have arisen on this subject? The amendments to the Constitution, and the laws under them, express the predominant opinion of those who conquered in the struggle, these amendments have a profound signification. To those who were but little concerned either in its chances or changes, and who were much interested in the financial opportunities it afforded, and were safe from its perils, these amendments are regarded very much as a party platform, whose value is exhausted at an election—as clouds without rain—trees without fruit—great swelling words to bring men into admiration for advantage.

In this very cause we have been charged with making a mock of those who made the amendment for their lax and reckless action, because we presume to assign a meaning, and to ground a claim for protection under the amendment. We do assign to this article of the amendment, and the thirteenth, of which it is the sequel and complement, a great and a weighty significance. We do not say that they make a radical change in the government of the United States, but they go very far to determine that the Constitution of the United States creates a national government and is not a federal compact.

The article determines who is a citizen of the United States' and that this person may become a citizen of any State by his own act—that condition being secondary and derivative from that constitution. It determines that the privileges and immunities of this citizen of all of the States—united, shall not be abridged by any one of them—nor shall any one of them deprive him of life, liberty or property, without due process of law; nor deny to him the equal protection of the laws.

Before these vested rights might be divested, slavery, and involuntary servitude existed under State constitutions; and the laws for the protection of life, liberty and property, were only, to a limited extent, subject to the revision of the judicial, or other departments of the United States. The fourteenth amendment to the constitution institutes a control over State sovereignty in the matter of life, liberty, property, privilege, immunity and equality....

BRIEF FOR DEFENDANTS—CHARLES ALLEN AND THOMAS DURANT, ATTORNEYS

Assuming, therefore, that the present charter would not be in violation of any provisions of the Constitution of the United States prior to the adoption of the 14th amendment, the question remains whether the adoption of that amendment involves the surrender, on the part of all the States, to the general Government, of all right of legislation of this character.

So far as can be judged by the public debates upon the subject, it was certainly never intended or contemplated that this amendment should receive such a construction. Have Congress and the whole nation been deceived, misled, mistaken? Have they done that which they did not intend to do?

Taken in the broadest sense, this provision (the 14th Amendment) would prohibit any State from abridging any existing privileges of any citizens of the United States, or from enforcing any law already enacted which abridges any privileges or immunities of citizens. It operates as a repeal of all laws which abridge privileges or immunities of citizens.

Taking it broadly, therefore, and this amendment will have the following results:

a. Repeal all laws imposing license fees upon any particular employments, lawful to pursue under the common law.

b. Repeal all laws regulating the mode of carrying on any lawful employments—all offensive or dangerous trades and articles.

c. Repeal all existing laws restraining the manufacture or sale of intoxicating liquors, restraining lotteries &c.

d. Repeal all existing laws as to the observance of the Lord's day, prohibiting labor or business thereon.

e. Repeal all existing laws regulating and fixing the hours of labor, and prohibiting the employment of children, women, or men in any particular occupations or places for more than a certain number of hours per day.

f. Repeal all existing charters and laws conferring exclusive privileges, heretofore adjudged constitutional and valid.

g. Prevent any legislature from passing any new statutes abridging the natural liberty of citizens in respect to any of these or kindred matters.

h. Bring within the jurisdiction of this court all questions relating to any of these or kindred subjects, and deprive the legislature and State courts of the several States to regulate and settle their internal affairs.

There is no occasion to give any such broad significance to the words "privileges and immunities."

It will probably not be contended for a moment that the 14th amendment should receive any such broad construction as would lead to the above results. It will no doubt be conceded that the legislatures of the several States may still regulate all these matters, and that the amendment to the Constitution was not designed to cover them, and does not cover them.

But, if that be so, on what just principles of construction can the amendment be held to render the present charter invalid? Shall it be held to apply to some acts of legislation, and not to others, though the latter are of the same general character?

In its nature, this charter relates solely to matters appropriate for what is sometimes called "municipal legislation," or "internal police." Will this court sit in judgment to determine whether, as an act of municipal legislation, it is reasonable in all its provisions?...

If this court is to determine these matters, and pronounce judgment whether the provisions of the charter are unreasonable, or the consideration inadequate, then will not the court take testimony upon the subject, to aid in arriving at a just conclusion? How can the court judicially know the exigency which will require the granting of such a charter? The legislature, by its committees and otherwise, inquires into the facts. How shall the court inform itself of the facts?

The result of the argument against the validity of this charter must, it would seem, be this: that the 14th amendment does not prohibit State legislatures from passing acts of municipal legislation which abridge the privileges and immunities of citizens, provided such acts appear to be reasonable, but does prohibit the passing of acts which appear to be unreasonable; that it is for this court to determine whether such acts are reasonable or unreasonable; and that this court will determine the question in each case, as it arises, simply upon a consideration of what appears on the face of the act, the validity of which is brought into question.

Such an argument is not supported by the true rules of constitutional construction....

It was considered proper by Congress on the suppression of the rebellion that new guards should be provided for the future peace and tranquillity of the country, and to effect this it was thought important to confer on the blacks the privileges enjoyed by the whites.

On the 9th April, 1866, Congress passed the act entitled "An act to protect all persons in the United States in their civil rights, and furnish the means of their vindication."

See 14 U.S. Statutes at Large, p. 27.

The same Congress, on the 16th June, 1866, passed the "Joint resolution proposing a fourteenth amendment to the Constitution of the United States."

14 Statutes, p. 358....

These two acts explain one another. They both have the same object in view. It was doubted whether the constitutional power of Congress extended to some of the matters embraced in the first section of April 9, hence the resolutions proposing constitutional amendment, which was designed to do nothing more than embody what the law had enacted, its adoption being rendered certain by the condition of accepting it being placed upon the States then recently in insurrection, by the reconstruction act of March 5, 1867.

The act and the amendment have no other meaning than to place the blacks on a footing of political and civil equality with the whites. A mischief existed, flowing from old relations, and to remedy that mischief was the design of the legislation of the time....

... Counsel of plaintiffs in error... contend that Congress and the States, who had at that time nothing more in mind than to confer equality of rights on the blacks, nevertheless went far beyond that, and have employed language which confers upon this court a jurisdiction over every case there can be imagined in every court of every State in the Union....

The occasion and the necessity, then, for the adoption of the fourteenth amendment was the constitutional status of the people of African descent, and if there had been no such people in the country, no such amendment would have been proposed. It was adopted for them. The contemporaneous discussions and debates at the time of the amendment show that no other object was in view, nor can it be made to embrace any other without sacrificing its spirit.

As the Constitution of the United States previous to 1867 prohibited any State from making one of African descent a citizen of the United States, and as to such alone the prohibition applied, the language of the amendment, however broad, applies to such only, and when it says that all persons born or naturalized in the United States are citizens of the United States and of the State wherein they reside, it can mean by all only the people of African descent, because all other people were already citizens of the United States, and beyond the scope of a constitutional amendment. It is a form of expression usual in the language of the Constitution, where people of African descent are always spoken of in similar terms....

The closing portion of the first section of the fourteenth amendment can have no meaning except as to persons of African descent, for in no State were any citizens ever subjected to any of the injuries, outrages, and disabilities denounced by the amendment.

If, by the exclusive privileges granted to the company, some natural rights in others are abridged, that abridgement results from the supremacy of the public welfare over individual interests.

Hence, if the fourteenth amendment forbids such legislation, it annuls all that is past, and prohibits all such in future.

It would be difficult to make a list, so numerous would be the instances; we may state canal charters, turnpike charters, bridge charters, railroad charters, gaslight company charters, and all others where, in consideration of public benefits derived, exclusive rights are conferred. We may further allude to acts for regulating the manufacture and storage of nitroglycerine, gunpowder, petroleum, and other dangerous substances; laws regulating lotteries and gift enterprises, fairs, markets, tanneries, and others of a like nature; laws regulating the labor in factories—as to the hours of work, age, and sex of the operatives; laws imposing licenses and taxes on trades, occupations, and professions; laws forbidding labor on the first day of the week; laws for the expropriation of private property to public use, and the numerous exclusive privileges enjoyed by political corporations.

All these must fall if this constitutional amendment means to constitute individual rights absolutely superior to the public welfare of the States in matters not political, and not touching the relation of the individual to the Government in his character of "citizen" of the United States.

The fourteenth amendment has no effect to confer any privileges and immunities which citizens of the United States did not enjoy before its adoption. It was designed to abrogate and render null all laws existing or which might be devised in the future making a distinction between white men and black as to privileges and immunities; and to show that the meaning is only such as those words conveyed in the past, they did not even confer the right of suffrage. To define accurately the words privileges and immunities, so as to embrace all the rights to be protected, would be impossible, but it is most manifest the design of the amendment was limited to the investiture of blacks with all the rights and immunities of whites, whatever these may be, and to protect them in their lives, liberties, and properties just as whites are protected. That is all that was and is necessary. To extend the interpretation of the Amendment to the length which the plaintiffs in error demand would break down the whole system of confederated State government, centralize the beautiful and harmonious system we enjoy into a consolidated and unlimited government, and render the Constitution of the United States, now the object of our love and veneration, as odious and insupportable as its enemies would wish to make it.

QUESTIONS

1. Campbell argues that the Fourteenth Amendment changed the entire relationship not only between the states and the federal government but, more important, between a citizen of a state and his state government. What evidence does he offer to support this claim?

2. Campbell notes that the federal Constitution goes very far toward determining the creation of a national government rather than a federal compact. Would this argument be any more valid in 1871 than in 1861? Why?

3. Campbell implies that the net result of the Louisiana statute involved in this case is to enslave a group of butchers. Do you agree? What evidence does Campbell offer to show that the framers had this type of "involuntary servitude" in mind when they adopted the Thirteenth and Fourteenth amendments?

4. Campbell writes that the Fourteenth Amendment was not adopted as an act of hostility toward various Southern states. Is there any evidence to indicate that the framers had hostile intentions toward the South when they drafted the amendment? If so, why does Campbell ignore it? What evidence does Campbell offer that the framers meant the amendment to apply to a group of butchers?

5. What does the Fourteenth Amendment state concerning the "right to labor"?

6. The lawyers for defendants—the state of Louisiana—noted some very significant differences between the courts and the legislature. What are they, and why do the lawyers discuss them?

7. According to Allen and Durant, what is the relationship between the Civil Rights Act of 1866 and the Fourteenth Amendment? What evidence is offered to support their viewpoint?

8. Allen and Durant claim that the key sections of the Fourteenth Amendment were supposed to apply only to people of African descent. What evidence do they present to support this contention?

9. On the basis of your understanding of the "intentions" of the amendment's framers, as well as of the words actually used, whose

arguments—Campbell's or Allen and Durant's—do you find to be more persuasive? Why?

The Slaughter-House Cases*

The majority in Slaughter-House *(the Court split 5 to 4) handed down an extremely important decision, for it cast the Fourteenth Amendment in a very narrow framework—one from which (more than one hundred years later) the amendment has not yet broken free.*

JUSTICE MILLER:
OPINION OF THE COURT

...The process of restoring to their proper relations with the Federal government and with the other States those who had sided with the rebellion, undertaken under the proclamation of President Johnson in 1865, and before the assembling of Congress, developed the fact that, notwithstanding the formal recognition by those States of the abolition of slavery, the condition of the slave race would, without further protection of the Federal government, be almost as bad as it was before. Among the first acts of legislation adopted by several of the States in the legislative bodies which claimed to be in their normal relations with the Federal government, were laws which imposed upon the colored race onerous disabilities and burdens, and curtailed their rights in the pursuit of life, liberty, and property to such an extent that their freedom was of little value, while they had lost the protection which they had received from their former owners from motives both of interest and humanity.

They were in some States forbidden to appear in the towns in any other character than menial servants. They were required to reside on and cultivate the soil without the right to purchase or own it. They were excluded from many occupations of gain, and were not permitted to give testimony in the courts in any case where a white man was a party. It was said that their lives were at the mercy of bad men, either because the laws for their protection were insufficient or were not enforced.

These circumstances, whatever, of falsehood or misconception may have been mingled with their presentation, forced upon the statesmen who had conducted the Federal government in safety through the crisis of the rebellion, and who supposed that by the thirteenth article of

* 16 Wall. 36, 71–82 (1873).

amendment they had secured the result of their labors, the conviction that something more was necessary in the way of constitutional protection to the unfortunate race who had suffered so much. They accordingly passed through Congress the proposition for the fourteenth amendment, and they declined to treat as restored to their full participation in the government of the Union the States which had been in insurrection, until they ratified that article by a formal vote of their legislative bodies. . . .

We repeat, then, in the light of this recapitulation of events, almost too recent to be called history, but which are familiar to us all; and on the most casual examination of the language of these amendments, no one can fail to be impressed with the one pervading purpose found in them all, lying at the foundation of each, and without which none of them would have been even suggested; we mean the freedom of the slave race, the security and firm establishment of that freedom, and the protection of the newly-made freeman and citizen from the oppressions of those who had formerly exercised unlimited dominion over him. It is true that only the fifteenth amendment, in terms, mentions the negro by speaking of his color and his slavery. But it is just as true that each of the other articles was addressed to the grievances of that race, and designed to remedy them as the fifteenth.

We do not say that no one else but the negro can share in this protection. Both the language and spirit of these articles are to have their fair and just weight in any question of construction. Undoubtedly while negro slavery alone was in the mind of the Congress which proposed the thirteenth article, it forbids any other kind of slavery, now or hereafter. If Mexican peonage or the Chinese coolie labor system shall develop slavery of the Mexican or Chinese race within our territory, this amendment may safely be trusted to make it void. And so if other rights are assailed by the States which properly and necessarily fall within the protection of these articles, that protection will apply, though the party interested may not be of African descent. But what we do say, and what we wish to be understood is, that in any fair and just construction of any section or phrase of these Amendments, it is necessary to look to the purpose which we have said was the pervading spirit of them all, the evil which they were designed to remedy, and the process of continued addition to the Constitution, until that purpose was supposed to be accomplished, as far as constitutional law can accomplish it. . . .

"All persons born or naturalized in the United States, and subject to the jurisdiction thereof, are citizens of the United States and of the State wherein they reside."

The first observation we have to make on this clause is, that it puts at rest both the questions which we stated to have been the subject of differences of opinion. It declares that persons may be citizens of the United States without regard to their citizenship of a particular State, and it overturns the Dred Scott decision by making all persons born within the United States and subject to its jurisdiction citizens of the United States. That its main purpose was to establish the citizenship of the negro can admit of no doubt. The phrase, "subject to its jurisdiction" was intended to exclude from its operation children of ministers, consuls, and citizens or subjects of foreign States born within the United States.

The next observation is more important in view of the arguments of counsel in the present case. It is, that the distinction between citizenship of the United States and citizenship of a State is clearly recognized and established. Not only may a man be a citizen of the United States without being a citizen of a State, but an important element is necessary to convert the former into the latter. He must reside within the State to make him a citizen of it, but it is only necessary that he should be born or naturalized in the United States to be a citizen of the Union.

It is quite clear, then, that there is a citizenship of the United States, and a citizenship of a State, which are distinct from each other, and which depend upon different characteristics or circumstances in the individual.

We think this distinction and its explicit recognition in this amendment of great weight in this argument, because the next paragraph of this same section, which is the one mainly relied on by the plaintiffs in error, speaks only of privileges and immunities of citizens of the United States, and does not speak of those of citizens of the several States. The argument, however, in favor of the plaintiffs rests wholly on the assumption that the citizenship is the same, and the privileges and immunities guaranteed by the clause are the same.

The language is, "No State shall make or enforce any law which shall abridge the privileges or immunities of citizens of the United States." It is a little remarkable, if this clause was intended as a protection to the citizen of a State against the legislative power of his own State, that the word citizen of the State should be left out when it is so carefully used, and used in contradistinction to citizens of the United States, in the very sentence which precedes it. It is too clear for argument that the change in phraseology was adopted understandingly and with a purpose.

Of the privileges and immunities of the citizen of the United States, and of the privileges and immunities of the citizen of the State, and what they respectively are, we will presently consider; but we wish to state here that it is only the former which are placed by this clause under the protection of the Federal Constitution, and that the latter, whatever they may be, are not intended to have any additional protection by this paragraph of the amendment

If, then, there is a difference between the privileges and immunities belonging to a citizen of the United States as such, and those belonging to the citizen of the State as such the latter must rest for their security and protection where they have heretofore rested; for they are not embraced by this paragraph of the amendment....

Was it the purpose of the fourteenth amendment, by the simple declaration that no State should make or enforce any law which shall abridge the privileges and immunities of citizens of the United States, to transfer the security and protection of all the civil rights which we have mentioned, from the States to the Federal government? And where it is declared that Congress shall have the power to enforce that article, was it intended to bring within the power of Congress the entire domain of civil rights heretofore belonging exclusively to the States?

All this and more must follow, if the proposition of the plaintiffs in error be sound. For not only are these rights subject to the control of Congress whenever in its discretion any of them are supposed to be abridged by State legislation, but that body may also pass laws in advance, limiting and restricting the exercise of legislative power by the States, in their most ordinary and usual functions, as in its judgment it may think proper on all such subjects. And still further, such a construction followed by the reversal of the judgments of the Supreme Court of Louisiana in these cases, would constitute this court a perpetual censor upon all legislation of the States, on the civil rights of their own citizens, with authority to nullify such as it did not approve as consistent with those rights, as they existed at the time of the adoption of this amendment. The argument we admit is not always the most conclusive which is drawn from the consequences urged against the adoption of a particular construction of an instrument. But when, as in the case before us, these consequences are so serious, so far-reaching and pervading, so great a departure from the structure and spirit of our institutions; when the effect is to fetter and degrade the State governments by subjecting them to the control of Congress, in the exercise of powers heretofore universally conceded to them of the most ordinary and fundamental character; when in fact it radically changes the whole theory of the relations of the State and Federal governments to each other and of both these governments to the people; the argument has a force that is irresistible, in the absence of language which expresses such a purpose too clearly to admit of doubt.

We are convinced that no such results were intended by the Congress which proposed these amendments, nor by the legislatures of the States which ratified them.

Having shown that the privileges and immunities relied on in the argument are those which belong to citizens of the States as such, and that they are left to the State governments for security and protection, and not by this article placed under the special care of the Federal government, we may hold ourselves excused from defining the privileges and immunities of citizens of the United States which no State can be abridge, until some case involving those privileges may make it necessary to do so....

In the early history of the organization of the government, its statesmen seem to have divided on the line which should separate the powers of the National government from those of the State governments, and though this line has never been very well defined in public opinion, such a division has continued from that day to this.

The adoption of the first eleven amendments to the Constitution so soon after the original instrument was accepted, shows a prevailing sense of danger at that time from the Federal power. And it cannot be denied that such a jealousy continued to exist with many patriotic men until the breaking out of the late civil war. It was then discovered that the true danger to the perpetuity of the Union was in the capacity of the State organizations to combine and concentrate all the powers of the State, and of contiguous States, for a determined resistance to the General Government.

Unquestionably this has given great force to the argument, and added largely to the number of those who believed in the necessity of a strong National government.

But, however pervading this sentiment, and however it may have contributed to the adoption of the amendments we have been considering, we do not see in those amendments any purpose to destroy the main features of the general system. Under the pressure of all the excited feeling growing out of the war, our statesmen have still believed that the existence of the States with powers for domestic and local government, including the regulation of civil rights—the rights of person and of property—was essential to the perfect working of our complex form of government, though they have thought proper to impose additional limitations on the States, and to confer power on that of the Nation....

JUSTICE FIELD, DISSENTING*

The act of Louisiana presents the naked case, unaccompanied by any public considerations, where a right to pursue a lawful and necessary calling, previously enjoyed by every citizen, and in connection with which a thousand persons were daily employed, is taken away and vested exclusively for twenty-five years, for an extensive district and a large population, in a single corporation, or its exercise is for that period restricted to the establishments of the corporation, and there allowed only upon onerous conditions.

If exclusive privileges of this character can be granted to a corporation of seventeen persons, they may, in the discretion of the legislature, be equally granted to a single individual. If they may be granted for twenty-five years they may be equally granted for a century, and in perpetuity. If they may be granted for the landing and keeping of animals intended for sale or slaughter they may be equally granted for the landing and storing of grain and other products of the earth, or for any article of commerce. If they may be granted for structures in which animal food is prepared for market they may be equally granted for structures in which farinaceous or vegetable food is prepared. They may be granted for any of the pursuits of human industry, even in its most simple and common forms. Indeed, upon the theory on which the exclusive privileges granted by the act in question are sustained, there is no monopoly, in the most odious form, which may not be upheld.

The question presented is, therefore, one of the greatest importance, not merely to the parties here, but to the whole country. It is nothing less than the question whether the recent amendments to the Federal Constitution protect the citizens of the United States against the deprivation of their common rights by State legislation. In my judgment the fourteenth amendment does afford such protection, and was so intended by the Congress which framed and the States which adopted it....

The terms, privileges and immunities, are not new in the amendment; they were in the Constitution before the amendment was adopted. They were found in the second section of the fourth article, which declares that "the citizens of each State shall be entitled to all privileges and immunities of citizens in the several States."...

It will not be pretended that under the fourth article of the

_____
* 16 Wall. 36, 88–89, 97, 101, 110 (1873).

Constitution any State could create a monopoly in any known trade or manufacture in favor of her own citizens, or any portion of them, which would exclude an equal participation in the trade or manufacture monopolized by citizens of other States. She could not confer, for example, upon any of her citizens the sole right to manufacture shoes, or boots, or silk, or the sole right to sell those articles in the State so as to exclude non-resident citizens from engaging in a similar manufacture or sale. The non-resident citizens could claim equality of privilege under the provisions of the fourth article with the citizens of the State exercising the monopoly as well as with others, and thus, as respects them, the monopoly would cease. If this were not so it would be in the power of the State to exclude at any time the citizens of other States from participation in particular branches of commerce or trade, and extend the exclusion from time to time so as effectually to prevent any traffic with them.

Now, what the clause in question does for the protection of citizens of one State against the creation of monopolies in favor of citizens of other States, the fourteenth amendment does for the protection of every citizen of the United States against the creation of any monopoly whatever. The privileges and immunities of citizens of the United States, of every one of them, is secured against abridgment in any form by any State. The fourteenth amendment places them under the guardianship of the National authority. All monopolies in any known trade or manufacture are an invasion of these privileges, for they encroach upon the liberty of citizens to acquire property and pursue happiness. . . .

The State may prescribe such regulations for every pursuit and calling of life as will promote the public health, secure the good order and advance the general prosperity of society, but when once prescribed, the pursuit or calling must be free to be followed by every citizen who is within the conditions designated, and will conform to the regulations. This is the fundamental idea upon which our institutions rest, and unless adhered to in the legislation of the country our government will be a republic only in name. The fourteenth amendment, in my judgment, makes it essential to the validity of the legislation of every State that this equality of right should be respected. How widely this equality has been departed from, how entirely rejected and trampled upon by the act of Louisiana, I have already shown. And it is to me a matter of profound regret that its validity is recognized by a majority of this court, for by it the right of free labor, one of the most sacred and imprescriptible rights of man, is violated.

JUSTICE BRADLEY, DISSENTING*

... The first section of [the Fourteenth] Amendment, after declaring that all persons born or naturalized in the United States, and subject to its jurisdiction, are citizens of the United States, and subject to its jurisdiction, are citizens of the United States and of the State wherein they reside, proceeds to declare further, that "no State shall make or enforce any law which shall abridge the privileges or immunities of citizens of the United States; nor shall any State deprive any person of life, liberty, or property, without due process of law, nor deny to any person within its jurisdiction the equal protection of the laws"; and that Congress shall have power to enforce by appropriate legislation the provisions of this article.

Now, here is a clear prohibition of the States against making or enforcing any law which shall abridge the privileges or immunities of citizens of the United States.

If my views are correct with regard to what are the privileges and immunities of citizens, it follows conclusively that any which establishes a sheer monopoly, depriving a large class of citizens of the privileges of pursuing a lawful employment, does abridge the privileges of those citizens.

The amendment also prohibits any State from depriving any person (citizen or otherwise) of life, liberty, or property, without due process of law.

In my view, a law which prohibits a large class of citizens from adopting a lawful employment, or from following a lawful employment previously adopted, does deprive them of liberty as well as property, without due process of law. Their right of choice is a portion of their liberty; their occupation is their property. Such a law also deprives those citizens of the equal protection of the laws, contrary to the last clause of the section.

The constitutional question is distinctly raised in these cases; the constitutional right is expressly claimed; it was violated by State law, which was sustained by the State court, and we are called upon in a legitimate and proper way to afford redress. Our jurisdiction and our duty are plain and imperative.

It is futile to argue that none but persons of the African race are intended to be benefited by this amendment. They may have been the

---

* 16 Wall. 36, 122–123 (1873).

primary cause of the amendment, but its language is general, embracing all citizens, and I think it was purposely so expressed.

The mischief to be remedied was not merely slavery and its incident and consequences; but that spirit of insubordination and disloyalty to the National government which had troubled the country for so many years in some of the States, and that intolerance of free speech and free discussion which often rendered life and property insecure, and led to much unequal legislation. The amendment was an attempt to give voice to the strong National yearning for that time and that condition of things, in which American citizenship should be a sure guaranty of safety, and in which every citizen of the United States might stand erect on every portion of its soil, in the full enjoyment of every right and privilege belonging to a freeman, without fear of violence or molestation.

But great fears are expressed that this construction of the amendment will lead to enactments by Congress interfering with the internal affairs of the States, and establishing therein civil and criminal codes of law for the governments in everything but name; or else, that it will lead the Federal courts to draw to their cognizance the supervision of State tribunals on every subject of judicial inquiry, on the plea of ascertaining whether the privileges and immunities of citizens have not been abridged.

In my judgment no such practical inconveniences would arise....

JUSTICE SWAYNE, DISSENTING*

These amendments are all consequences of the late civil war. The prejudices and apprehension as to the central government which prevailed when the Constitution was adopted were dispelled by the light of experience. The public mind became satisfied that there was less danger of tyranny in the head than of anarchy and tyranny in the members. The provisions of this section are all eminently conservative in their character. They are a bulwark of defence, and can never be made an engine of oppression. The language employed is unqualified in its scope. There is no exception in its terms, and there can be properly none in their application. By the language "citizens of the United States" was meant all such citizens; and by "any person" was meant all persons within the jurisdiction of the State. No distinction is intimated on

* 16 Wall. 36, 128–129 (1873).

account of race or color. This court has no authority to interpolate a limitation that is neither expressed nor implied. Our duty is to execute the law, not to make it. The protection provided was not intended to be confined to those of any particular race or class, but to embrace equally all races, classes, and conditions of men. It is objected that the power conferred is novel and large. The answer is that the novelty was known and the measure deliberately adopted. The power is beneficent in its nature, and cannot be abused. It is such as should exist in every well-ordered system of polity. Where could it be more appropriately lodged than in the hands to which it is confided? It is necessary to enable the government of the nation to secure to every one within its jurisdiction the rights and privileges enumerated, which, according to the plainest considerations of reason and justice and the fundamental principles of the social compact, all are entitled to enjoy. Without such authority any government claiming to be national is glaringly defective. The construction adopted by the majority of my brethren is, in my judgment, much too narrow. It defeats, by a limitation not anticipated, the intent of those by whom the instrument was framed and of those by whom it was adopted. To the extent of that limitation it turns, as it were, what was meant for bread into a stone. By the Constitution, as it stood before the war, ample protection was given against oppression by the Union, but little was given against wrong and oppression by the State. That want was intended to be supplied by this amendment. Against the former this court has been called upon more than once to interpose. Authority of the same amplitude was intended to be conferred as to the latter. But this arm of our jurisdiction is, in these cases, stricken down by the judgment just given. Nowhere, than in this court ought the will of the nation, as thus expressed, to be more liberally construed or more cordially executed. This determination of the majority seems to me to lie far in the other direction.

QUESTIONS

1.   In a major constitutional case such as this, how heavily did Justice Miller rely on arguments of counsel? Did the Court break new ground with this decision? Or did it merely ratify, not innovate?

2.   Do you find Miller's use of history convincing? What evidence does he cite?

3.   For Miller, which appears more important—the intentions of the framers or the words that they actually used in the Fourteenth Amendment?

4. For Justices Field, Bradley, and Swayne, would your answer be different? Why?

5. In what sense might it be said that in *Slaughter-House* the majority looked backward to what once had been, while the minority looked forward toward what was yet to come?

*The Civil Rights Cases**

JUSTICE BRADLEY: OPINION OF THE COURT

It is State action of a particular character that is prohibited. Individual invasion of individual rights is not the subject matter of the [Fourteenth] amendment. It has a deeper and broader scope. It nullifies and makes void all State legislation, and State action of every kind, which impairs the privileges and immunities of citizens of the United States, or which injures them in life, liberty or property without due process of law, or which denies to any of them the equal protection of the laws. It not only does this, but, . . . the amendment invests Congress with power to enforce it by appropriate legislation. To enforce what? To enforce the prohibition. To adopt appropriate legislation for correcting the effects of such prohibited State laws and State acts, and thus to render them effectually null, void, and innocuous. This is the legislative power conferred upon Congress, and this is the whole of it. It does not invest Congress with power to legislate upon subjects which are within the domain of State legislation; but to provide modes of relief against State legislation, or State action, of the kind referred to. . . .

And so in the present case, until some State law has been passed, or some State action through its officers or agents has been taken, adverse to the rights of citizens sought to be protected by the Fourteenth Amendment, no legislation of the United States under said amendment, nor any proceeding under such legislation, can be called into activity: for the prohibitions of the amendment are against State laws and acts done under State authority. Of course, legislation may, and should be, provided in advance to meet the exigency when it arises; but it should be adapted to the mischief and wrong which the amendment was intended to provide against; and that is, State laws, or State action of some kind, adverse to the rights of the citizen secured by the amendment. . . .

* 109 U.S. 3, 11, 13-14, 23-25 (1883).

An inspection of the law shows that it makes no reference whatever to any supposed or apprehended violation of the Fourteenth Amendment on the part of the States. It is not predicated on any such view. It proceeds *ex-directo* to declare that certain acts committed by individuals shall be deemed offences, and shall be prosecuted and punished by proceedings in the courts of the United States. It does not profess to be corrective of any constitutional wrong committed by the States; it does not make its operation to depend upon any such wrong committed. It applies equally to cases arising in States which have the justest laws respecting the personal rights of citizens, and whose authorities are ever ready to enforce such laws, as to those which arise in States that may have violated the prohibition of the amendment. In other words, it steps into the domain of local jurisprudence, and lays down rules for the conduct of individuals in society towards each other, and imposes sanctions for the enforcement of those rules, without referring in any manner to any supposed action of the State or its authorities.

If this legislation is appropriate for enforcing the prohibitions of the amendment, it is difficult to see where it is to stop. Why may not Congress with equal show of authority enact a code of laws for the enforcement and vindication of all rights of life, liberty, and property? If it is supposable that the States may deprive persons of life, liberty, and property without due process of law (and the amendment itself does suppose this), why should not Congress proceed at once to prescribe due process of law for the protection of every one of these fundamental rights, in every possible case, as well as to prescribe equal privileges in inns, public conveyances, and theatres? The truth is, that the implication of a power to legislate in this manner is based upon the assumption that if the States are forbidden to legislate or act in a particular way on a particular subject, and power is conferred upon Congress to enforce the prohibition, this gives Congress power to legislate generally upon that subject, and not merely power to provide modes of redress against such State legislature or action. The assumption is certainly unsound. . . .

. . . The only question under the present head, therefore, is, whether the refusal to any persons of the accommodations of an inn, or a public conveyance, or a place of public amusement, by an individual, and without any sanction or support from any State law or regulation, does inflict upon such persons any manner of servitude, or form of slavery, as those terms are understood in this country? Many wrongs may be obnoxious to the prohibitions of the Fourteenth Amendment which are not, in any just sense, incidents or elements of slavery. Such, for example, would be the taking of private property without due process of law; or allowing persons who have committed certain crimes (horse stealing, for example) to be seized and hung by the posse comitatus without regular trial; or denying to any person, or class of persons, the right to pursue any peaceful avocations allowed to others. What is called class legislation would belong to this category, and would be obnoxious to the prohibitions of the Fourteenth Amendment, but would not necessarily be so to the Thirteenth, when not involving the idea of any subjection of one man to another. The Thirteenth Amendment has respect, not to distinctions of race, or class, or color, but to slavery. The Fourteenth Amendment extends its protection to races and classes, and prohibits any State legislation which has the effect of denying to any race or class, or to any individual, the equal protection of the laws.

Now, conceding, for the sake of the argument, that the admission to an inn, a public conveyance, or a place of public amusement, on equal terms with all other citizens, is the right of every man and all classes of men, is it any more than one of those rights which the states by the Fourteenth Amendment are forbidden to deny to any person? And is the Constitution violated until the denial of the right has some State sanction or authority? Can the act of a mere individual, the owner of the inn, the public conveyance or place of amusement, refusing the accommodation, be justly regarded as imposing any badge of slavery or servitude upon the applicant, or only as inflicting an ordinary civil injury, properly cognizable by the laws of the State, and presumably subject to redress by those laws until the contrary appears?

After giving to these questions all the consideration which their importance demands, we are forced to the conclusion that such an act of refusal has nothing to do with slavery or involuntary servitude, and that if it is violative of any right of the party, his redress is to be sought under the laws of the State; or if those laws are adverse to his rights and do not protect him, his remedy will be found in the corrective legislation which Congress has adopted, or may adopt, for counteracting the effect of State laws, or State action, prohibited by the Fourteenth Amendment. It would be running the slavery argument into the ground to make it apply to every act of discrimination which a person may see fit to make as to the guests he will entertain, or as to the people he will take into his coach or cab or car, or admit to this concert or theatre, or deal with in other matters of intercourse or business. Innkeepers and public carriers, by the laws of all the States, so far as we are aware, are bound, to the extent of their facilities, to furnish proper accommodation to all unobjectionable persons who in good faith apply for them. If the laws themselves make any unjust discrimination, amenable to the prohibitions of the Fourteenth Amendment, Congress has full power to afford a remedy under that amendment and in accordance with it.

JUSTICE HARLAN, DISSENTING*

The opinion in these cases proceeds, it seems to me, upon grounds entirely too narrow and artificial. I cannot resist the conclusion that the substance and spirit of the recent amendments of the Constitution have been sacrified by a subtle and ingenious verbal criticism. "It is not the words of the law but the internal sense of it that makes the law: the letter of the law is the body; the sense and reason of the law is the soul." Constitutional provisions, adopted in the interest of liberty, and for the purpose of securing, through national legislation, if need be, rights inhering in a state of freedom, and belonging to American citizenship, have been so construed as to defeat the ends the people desired to accomplish, which they attempted to accomplish, and which they supposed they had accomplished by changes in their fundamental law....

Remembering that this court, in the Slaughter-House Cases, declared that the one pervading purpose found in all the recent amendments, lying at the foundation of each, and without which none of them would have been suggested—was "the freedom of the slave race, the security and firm establishment of that freedom, and the protection of the newly-made freeman and citizen from the oppression of those who had formerly exercised unlimited dominion over him"—that each amendment was addressed primarily to the grievances of that race—let us proceed to consider the language of the Fourteenth Amendment....

The assumption that this amendment consists wholly of prohibitions upon State laws and State proceedings in hostility to its provisions, is unauthorized by its language. The first clause of the first section—"All persons born or naturalized in the United States, and subject to the jurisdiction thereof, are citizens of the United States, and of the State wherein they reside"—is of a distinctly affirmative character. In its application to the colored race, previously liberated, it created and granted, as well citizenship of the United States, as citizenship of the State in which they respectively resided. It introduced all of that race,

* 109 U.S. 3, 26, 44, 46, 52–53, 59–61 (1883).

whose ancestors had been imported and sold as slaves, at once, into the political community known as the "People of the United States." They became, instantly, citizens of the United States, and of their respective States. Further they were brought, by this supreme act of the nation, within the direct operation of that provision of the Constitution which declares that "the citizens of each State shall be entitled to all privileges and immunities of citizens in the several States." Art. 4, § 2. . . .

The opinion of the court, as I have said, proceeds upon the ground that the power of Congress to legislate for the protection of the rights and privileges secured by the Fourteenth Amendment cannot be brought into activity except with the view, and as it may become necessary, to correct and annul State laws and State proceedings in hostility to such rights and privileges. In the absence of State laws or State action adverse to such rights and privileges, the nation may not actively interfere for their protection and security, even against corporations and individuals exercising public or quasipublic functions. Such I understand to be the position of my brethren. If the grant to colored citizens of the United States of citizenship in their respective States, imports exemption from race discrimination, in their States, in respect of such civil rights as belong to citizenship, then, to hold that the amendment remits that right to the States for their protection, primarily, and stays the hands of the nation, until it is assailed by State laws or State proceedings, is to adjudge that the amendment, so far from enlarging the powers of Congress—as we have heretofore said it did—not only curtails them, but reverses the policy which the general government has pursued from its very organization. Such an interpretation of the amendment is a denial to Congress of the power, by appropriate legislation, to enforce one of its provisions. In view of the circumstances under which the recent amendments were incorporated into the Constitution, and especially in view of the peculiar character of the new rights they created and secured, it ought not to be presumed that the general government has abdicated its authority, by national legislation, direct and primary in its character, to guard and protect privileges and immunities secured by that instrument. Such an interpretation of the Constitution ought not to be accepted if it be possible to avoid it. Its acceptance would lead to this anomalous result: that whereas, prior to the amendments, Congress, with the sanction of this court, passed the most stringent laws—operating directly and primarily upon States and their officers and agents, as well as upon individuals—in vindication of slavery and the right of the master, it may not now, by legislation of a like primary and direct character, guard, protect, and secure the freedom established, and the most essential right of the citizenship granted, by the constitutional amendments. With all respect for the opinion of others, I insist that the national legislature may, without transcending the limits of the Constitution, do for human liberty and the fundamental rights of American citizenship, what it did, with the sanction of this court, for the protection of slavery and rights of the masters of fugitive slaves. If fugitive slave laws, providing modes and prescribing penalties, whereby the master could seize and recover his fugitive slave, were legitimate exercises of an implied power to protect and enforce a right recognized by the Constitution, why shall the hands of Congress be tied, so that—under an express power, by appropriate legislation, to enforce a constitutional provision granting citizenship—it may not, by means of direct legislation, bring the whole power of this nation to bear upon States and their officers, and upon such individuals and corporations exercising public functions as assume to abridge, impair, or deny rights confessedly secured by the supreme law of the land? . . .

I agree that government has nothing to do with social, as distinguished from technically legal, rights of individuals. No government ever has brought, or ever can bring, its people into social intercourse against their wishes. Whether one person will permit or maintain social relations with another is a matter with which government has no concern. I agree that if one citizen chooses not to hold social intercourse with another, he is not and cannot be made amenable to the law for his conduct in that regard; for even upon grounds of race, no legal right of a citizen is violated by the refusal of others to maintain merely social relations with him. What I affirm is that no State, nor the officers of any State, nor any corporation or individual wielding power under State authority for the public benefit or the public convenience, can, consistently either with the freedom established by the fundamental law, or with that equality of civil rights which now belongs to every citizen, discriminate against freemen or citizens, in those rights, because of their race, or because they once labored under the disabilities of slavery imposed upon them as a race. The rights which Congress, by the act of 1875, endeavored to secure and protect are legal, not social rights. The right, for instance, of a colored citizen to use the accommodations of a public highway, upon the same terms as are permitted to white citizens, is no more a social right than his right, under the law, to use the public streets of a city or a town, or a turnpike road, or a public market, or a post office, or his right to sit in a public building with others, of whatever race, for the purpose of hearing the political questions of the day discussed. Scarcely a day passes without our seeing in this court-room citizens of the white and black races sitting side by side, watching the progress of our business. It would never occur to any one that the presence of a colored citizen in a court-house, or court-room, was an invasion of the social rights of white persons who may frequent such places. And yet, such a suggestion would be quite as sound in law—I say it with all respect—as is the suggestion that the claim of a colored citizen to use, upon the same terms as is permitted to white citizens, the accommodations of public highways, or public inns, or places of public amusement, established under the license of the law, is an invasion of the social rights of the white race....

My brethren say, that when a man has emerged from slavery, and by the aid of beneficent legislation has shaken off the inseparable concomitants of that state, there must be some stage in the progress of his elevation when he takes the rank of a mere citizen, and ceases to be the special favorite of the laws, and when his rights as a citizen, or a man, are to be protected in the ordinary modes by which other men's rights are protected. It is, I submit, scarcely just to say that the colored race has been the special favorite of the laws. The statute of 1875, now adjudged to be unconstitutional, is for the benefit of citizens of every race and color. What the nation, through Congress, has sought to accomplish in reference to that race is—what had already been done in every State of the Union for the white race—to secure and protect rights belonging to them as freemen and citizens; nothing more. It was not deemed enough "to help the feeble up, but to support him after." The one underlying purpose of congressional legislation has been to enable the black race to take the rank of mere citizens, and to secure the enjoyment of privileges belonging, under the law, to them as a component part of the people for whose welfare and happiness government is ordained.

QUESTIONS

1.   What is the distinction that Justice Bradley draws between *corrective* as opposed to *primary* or *direct* legislation? Do you find it convincing? Do you think it accords with the *intentions* of the framers? What does Bradley's interpretation do to the scope of the Fourteenth Amendment?

2.   What is the distinction that Justice Harlan draws between *legal*

as opposed to *social* rights? Would Bradley reject this distinction? Does Harlan actually confront the arguments raised by Bradley in his opinion for the Court?

3.   Do these two opinions offer us any insights into the relationship between law and change? What do you think ought to be a "proper" relationship between these two forces?

4.   A says: "The Constitution is what the judges say it is." B says: "The Constitution is what the words in it actually mean." Who is correct, A or B?

*Plessy v. Ferguson**

JUSTICE BROWN: OPINION OF THE COURT

... We consider the underlying fallacy of the plaintiff's argument to consist in the assumption that the enforced separation of the two races stamps the colored race with a badge of inferiority. If this be so, it is not by reason of anything found in the act, but solely because the colored race chooses to put that construction upon it. The argument necessarily assumes that if, as has been more than once the case, and is not unlikely to be so again, the colored race should become the dominant power in the state legislature, and should enact a law in precisely similar terms, it would thereby relegate the white race to an inferior position. We imagine that the white race, at least, would not acquiesce in this assumption. The argument also assumes that social prejudices may be overcome by legislation, and that equal rights cannot be secured to the negro except by an enforced commingling of the two races. We cannot accept this proposition. If the two races are to meet on terms of social equality, it must be the result of natural affinities, a mutual appreciation of each other's merits and a voluntary consent of individuals. ... Legislation is powerless to eradicate racial instincts or to abolish distinctions based upon physical differences, and the attempt to do so can only result in accentuating the difficulties of the present situation. If the civil and political rights of both races be equal, one cannot be inferior to the other civially or politically. If one race be inferior to the other socially, the Constitution of the United States cannot put them upon the same plane.

* 163 U.S. 537, 551–552 (1896).

JUSTICE HARLAN, DISSENTING*

Justice Harlan's dissent in this case is regarded as one of the greatest in his long career. A colleague once described Harlan as one who slept at night with one hand on the Constitution and the other on the Bible, thus sleeping the sweet sleep of righteousness.

It is one thing for railroad carriers to furnish, or to be required by law to furnish, equal accommodations for all whom they are under a legal duty to carry. It is quite another thing for government to forbid citizens of the white and black races from traveling in the same public conveyance, to punish officers of railroad companies for permitting persons of the two races to occupy the same passenger coach. If a state can prescribe as a rule of civil conduct, that whites and blacks shall not travel as passengers in the same railroad coach, why may it not so regulate the use of the streets of its cities and towns as to compel white citizens to keep on one side of the street and black citizens to keep on the other? Why may it not, upon like grounds, punish whites and blacks who ride together in street cars or in open vehicles on a public road or street? Why may it not require sheriffs to assign whites to one side of a court-room and blacks to the other? And why may it not also prohibit the commingling of the two races in the galleries of legislative halls or in public assemblages convened for the political question of the day? Further, if this statute of Louisiana is consistent with the personal liberty of citizens, why may not the state require the separation in railroad coaches of native and naturalized citizens of the United States, or of Protestants and Roman Catholics? . . .

The white race deems itself to be the dominant race in this country. And so it is, in prestige, in achievements, in education, in wealth, and in power. So, I doubt not that it will continue to be for all time, if it remains true to its great heritage and holds fast to the principles of constitutional liberty. But in view of the Constitution, in the eye of the law, there is in this country no superior, dominant, ruling class of citizens. There is no caste here. Our Constitution is color-blind, and neither knows nor tolerates classes among citizens. In respect of civil rights, all citizens are equal before the law. The humblest is the peer of the most powerful. The law regards man as man, and takes no account of his surroundings or of his color when his civil rights as guaranteed by the supreme law of the land are involved. It is therefore to be regretted that this high tribunal,

* 163 U.S. 537, 557, 559–562 (1896).

the final expositor of the fundamental law of the land, has reached the conclusion that it is competent for a state to regulate the enjoyment by citizens of their civil rights solely upon the basis of race.

In my opinion, the judgment this day rendered will, in time, prove to be quite as pernicious as the decision made by this tribunal in the Dred Scott Case. It was adjudged in that case that the descendants of Africans who were imported into this country and sold as slaves were not included nor intended to be included under the word "citizens" in the Constitution, and could not claim any of the rights and privileges which that instrument provided for and secured to citizens of the United States; that at the time of the adoption of the Constitution they were "considered as a subordinate and inferior class of beings, who had been subjugated by the dominant race, and, whether emancipated or not, yet remained subject to their authority, and had no rights or privileges but such as those who held the power and the government might choose to grant them." 60 U.S. 393, 404; 19 How. 393, 404. The recent amendments of the Constitution, it was supposed, had eradicated these principles from our institutions. But it seems that we have yet, in some of the states, a dominant race, a superior class of citizens, which assumes to regulate the enjoyment of civil rights, common to all citizens, upon the basis of race. The present decision, it may well be apprehended, will not stimulate aggressions, more or less brutal and irritating, upon the admitted rights of colored citizens, but will encourage the belief that it is possible, by means of state enactments, to defeat the beneficent purposes which the people of the United States had in view when they adopted the recent amendments of the Constitution, by one of which the blacks of this country were made citizens of the United States and of the states in which they respectively reside and whose privileges and immunities, as citizens, the states are forbidden to abridge. Sixty millions of whites are in no danger from the presence here of eight millions of blacks. The destinies of the two races in this country are indissolubly linked together, and the interests of both require that the common government of all shall not permit the seeds of race hate to be planted under the sanction of law. What can more certainly arouse race hate, what more certainly create and perpetuate a feeling of distrust between these races, than state enactments which in fact proceed on the ground that colored citizens are so inferior and degraded that they cannot be allowed to sit in public coaches occupied by white citizens? That, as all will admit, is the real meaning of such legislation as was enacted in Louisiana.

The sure guaranty of the peace and security of each race is the clear, distinct, unconditional recognition by our governments, national and state, of every right that inheres in civil freedom, and of the equality before the law of all citizens of the United States without regard to race. State enactments, regulating the enjoyment of civil rights, upon the basis of race, and cunningly devised to defeat legitimate results of the war, under the pretense of recognizing equality of rights, can have no other result than to render permanent peace impossible and to keep alive a conflict of races, the continuance of which must do harm to all concerned. This question is not met by the suggestion that social equality cannot exist between the white and black races in this country. That argument, if it can be properly regarded as one, is scarcely worthy of consideration, for social equality no more exists between two races when traveling in a passenger coach or a public highway than when members of the same races sit by each other in a street car or in the jury box, or stand or sit with each other in a political assembly, or when they use in common the streets of a city or town, or when they are in the same room for the purpose of having their names placed on the registry of voters, or when they approach the ballot-box in order to exercise the high privilege of voting.

There is a race so different from our own that we do not permit those belonging to it to become citizens of the United States. Persons belonging to it are, with few exceptions, absolutely excluded from our country. I allude to the Chinese race. But by the statute in question a Chinaman can ride in the same passenger coach with white citizens of the United States, while citizens of the black race in Louisiana, many of whom, perhaps, risked their lives for the preservation of the Union, who are entitled by law to participate in the political control of the state and nation, who are not excluded, by law or by reason of their race, from public stations of any kind, and who have all the legal rights that belong to white citizens, are yet declared to be criminals, liable to imprisonment, if they ride in a public coach occupied by citizens of the white race. It is scarcely just to say that a colored citizen should not object to occupying a public coach assigned to his own race. He does not object, nor, perhaps, would he object to separate coaches for his race, if his rights under the law were recognized. But he does object, and he ought never to cease objecting, that citizens of the white and black races can be adjudged criminals because they sit, or claim the right to sit, in the same public coach on a public highway.

The arbitrary separation of citizens, on the basis of race, while they are on a public highway, is a badge of servitude wholly inconsistent with the civil freedom and the equality before the law established by the Constitution. It cannot be justified upon any legal grounds.

If evils will result from the commingling of the two races upon public highways established for the benefit of all, they will be infinitely less than those that will surely come from state legislation regulating the enjoyment of civil rights upon the basis of race. We boast of the freedom enjoyed by our people above all other peoples. But it is difficult to reconcile that boast with a state of the law which, practically, puts the brand of servitude and degredation upon a large class of our fellow citizens, our equals before the law. The thin disguise of "equal" accommodations for passengers in railroad coaches will not mislead anyone, or atone for the wrong this day done....

QUESTIONS

1. Harlan states that a colored citizen "does not object, nor, perhaps, would he object to separate coaches for his race, if his rights under the law were recognized." What does he mean?
2. What rights is he referring to?
3. Does his contention seem inconsistent with his other points? Why or why not?

United States v. Cruikshank: *Brief on Behalf of the United States**

In 1870, Congress responded to growing evidence of violence and intimidation against blacks in sections of the South by passing an "enforcement act." Convictions obtained under this statute were challenged before the United States Supreme Court in the case of United States v. Cruikshank, *where they were reversed.*

...A *conspiracy* may be an offense against the United States. If it be to do something which directly concerns the United States, and if it have been made criminal by statute, it is within Federal jurisdiction.

Although it be to do something which directly concerns the United States, it is not within Federal criminal jurisdiction unless itself made criminal by statute, as there is no common law of crime under the United States.

* *Landmark Briefs and Arguments,* vol. 7, pp. 292–294.

But where Congress has enacted that a combination to effect an object which directly concerns the United States shall be criminal, nothing material occurs to us to suggest that such legislation is not both competent and proper.... Congress has enacted *that if two or more persons shall band or conspire together with intent to injure, oppress, threaten, or intimidate any citizen with intent to prevent or hinder his free exercise of any right or privilege granted or secured to him by the Constitution or laws of the United States, such person shall be held guilty of felony, &c.*

We might content ourselves here with saying that inasmuch as the XIVth amendment to the Constitution established the relation of citizenship, and confers upon Congress the power to enforce that relation by suitable legislation, it seems plain that if such *citizenship* be not merely a *sound,* signifying nothing; if it include political and other "rights and privileges" *respecting the Government of the United States,* this amendment empowers and *thus makes it the duty of Congress* to legislate so as to enforce those rights and privileges, whether by protection against criminal assault or otherwise.

This is an expression and a fresh signification of the will of the people of the United States upon this point, but it is not the origin of that *duty,* for it seems that this statute would have been constitutional *at any time since* 1789, as regards the right to vote in Federal elections; the right to resort to the protection of Federal courts; the right to hold Federal offices; the right to inter-state and foreign *commerce;* and the right to assemble and consult about Federal politics, and to petition Congress for redress of Federal grievances. (Slaughter-House cases. 16 Wall., p. 79.)

As these rights owe their existence to the Federal Government, and as, *vice versa,* the Federal Government owes its value, if not its existence, very much to their exercise, it seems that nothing can be said to impeach the validity of Federal legislation to protect them against any opposer. Such protection seems indeed to raise not so much a question of POWER in the United States, as of DUTY....

United States v. Cruikshank*

Speaking for a unanimous Court, Chief Justice Waite (described by one observer as "a respectable nobody") did not actually declare the statute unconstitutional, but rather insisted that any indictments based on it had to deal with offenses punishable under federal law. Such, he found, was not the case in the indictments at issue here.

CHIEF JUSTICE WAITE: OPINION OF THE COURT

This case . . . presents for our consideration an indictment containing sixteen counts, divided into two series of eight counts each, based upon sect. 6 of the Enforcement Act of May 31, 1870. That section is as follows:

> "That if two or more persons shall band or conspire together, or go in disguise upon the public highway, or upon the premises of another, with intent to violate any provision of this act, or to injure, oppress, threaten, or intimidate any citizen, with intent to prevent or hinder his free exercise and enjoyment of any right or privilege granted or secured to him by the constitution or laws of the United States, or because of his having exercised the same, such persons shall be held guilty of felony, and, on conviction thereof, shall be fined or imprisoned, or both, at the discretion of the court,—the fine not to exceed $5,000, and the imprisonment not to exceed ten years; and shall, moreover, be thereafter ineligible to, and disabled from holding, any office or place of honor, profit, or trust created by the constitution or laws of the United States." 16 Stat. 141. . . .

The general charge in the first eight counts is that of "banding," and in the second eight, that of "conspiring" together to injure, oppress, threaten, and intimidate Levi Nelson and Alexander Tillman, citizens of the United States, of African descent and persons of color, with the intent thereby to hinder and prevent them in their free exercise and enjoyment of rights and privileges "granted and secured" to them "in common with all other good citizens of the United States by constitution and laws of the United States."

The offences provided for by the statute in question do not consist in the mere "banding" or "conspiring" of two or more persons together, but in their banding or conspiring with the intent, or for any of the

---

*92 U.S. 542, 548–555 (1875).

purposes, specified. To bring this case under the operation of the statute, therefore, it must appear that the right, the enjoyment of which the conspirators intended to hinder or prevent, was one granted or secured by the constitution or laws of the United States. If it does not so appear, the criminal matter charged has not been made indictable by any act of Congress.

We have in our political system a government of the United States and a government of each of the several States. Each one of these governments is distinct from the others, and each has citizens of its own who owe it allegiance, and whose rights, within its jurisdiction, it must protect. The same person may be at the same time a citizen of the United States and a citizen of a State, but his rights of citizenship under one of these governments will be different from those he has under the other.

Citizens are the members of the political community to which they belong. They are the people who compose the community, and who, in their associated capacity, have established or submitted themselves to the dominion of a government for the promotion of their general welfare and the protection of their individual as well as their collective rights. In the formation of a government, the people may confer upon it such powers as they choose. The government, when so formed, may, and when called upon should, exercise all the powers it has for the protection of the rights of its citizens and the people within its jurisdiction; but it can exercise no other. The duty of a government to afford protection is limited always by the power it possesses for that purpose.

Experience made the fact known to the people of the United States that they required a national government for national purposes. The separate governments of the separate States, bound together by the articles of confederation alone, were not sufficient for the promotion of the general welfare of the people in respect to foreign nations, or for their complete protection as citizens of the confederated States. For this reason, the people of the United States, "in order to form a more perfect union, establish justice, insure domestic tranquillity, provide for the common defence, promote the general welfare, and secure the blessings of liberty" to themselves and their posterity (Const. Preamble), ordained and established the government of the United States, and defined its powers by a constitution, which they adopted as its fundamental law, and made its rule of action.

The government thus established and defined is to some extent a government of the States in their political capacity. It is also, for certain purposes, a government of the people. Its powers are limited in number, but not in degree. Within the scope of its powers, as enumerated and defined, it is supreme and above the States; but beyond, it has no existence. It was erected for special purposes, and endowed with all powers necessary for its own preservation and the accomplishment of the ends its people had in view. It can neither grant nor secure to its citizens any right or privilege not expressly or by implication placed under its jurisdiction.

The people of the United States resident within any State are subject to two governments: one State, and the other National; but there need be no conflict between the two. The powers which one possesses, the other does not. They are established for different purposes, and have separate jurisdictions. Together they make one whole, and furnish the people of the United States with a complete government, ample for the protection of all their rights at home and abroad. True, it may sometimes happen that a person is amenable to both jurisdictions for one and the same act. Thus, if a marshal of the United States is unlawfully resisted while executing the process of the courts within a State, and the resistance is accompanied by an assault on the officer, the sovereignty of the United States is violated by the resistance, and that of the State by the breach of peace, in the assault. So, too, if one passes counterfeited coin of the United States within a State, it may be an offence against the United States and the State: The United States, because it discredits the coin; and the State, because of the fraud upon him to whom it is passed. This does not, however, necessarily imply that the two governments possess powers in common, or bring them into conflict with each other. It is the natural consequence of a citizenship which owes allegiance to two sovereignties, and claims protection from both. The citizen cannot complain, because he has voluntarily submitted himself to such a form of government. He owes allegiance to the two departments, so to speak, and within their respective spheres must pay the penalties which each exacts for disobedience to its laws. In return, he can demand protection from each within its own jurisdiction.

The government of the United States is one of delegated powers alone. Its authority is defined and limited by the Constitution. All powers not granted to it by that instrument are reserved to the States or the people. No rights can be acquired under the constitution or laws of the United States, except such as the government of the United States has authority to grant or secure. All that cannot be so granted or secured are left under the protection of the States.

We now proceed to an examination of the indictment, to ascertain whether the several rights, which it is alleged the defendants intended to interfere with, are such as had been in law and in fact granted or secured by the constitution or laws of the United States.

The first and ninth counts state the intent of the defendants to have been to hinder and prevent the citizens named in the free exercise and enjoyment of their "lawful right and privilege to peaceably assemble together with each other and with other citizens of the United States for a peaceful and lawful purpose." The right of the people peaceably to assemble for lawful purposes existed long before the adoption of the Constitution of the United States. In fact, it is, and always has been, one of the attributes of citizenship under a free government. It "derives its source," to use the language of Chief Justice Marshall, in *Gibbons v. Ogden,* 9 Wheat. 211, "from those laws whose authority is acknowledged by civilized man throughout the world." It is found wherever civilization exists. It was not, therefore, a right granted to the people by the Constitution. The government of the United States when established found it in existence, with the obligation on the part of the States to afford it protection. As no direct power over it was granted to Congress, it remains, according to the ruling in *Gibbons v. Ogden,* id. 203, subject to State jurisdiction. Only such existing rights were committed by the people to the protection of Congress as came within the general scope of the authority granted to the national government.

The first amendment to the Constitution prohibits Congress from abridging "the right of the people to assemble and to petition the government for a redress of grievances." This, like the other amendments proposed and adopted at the same time, was not intended to limit the powers of the State governments in respect to their own citizens, but to operate upon the National government alone.... It is now too late to question the correctness of this construction. As was said by the late Chief Justice, in *Twitchell v. The Commonwealth,* 7 Wall. 325, "the scope and application of these amendments are no longer subjects of discussion here." They left the authority of the States just where they found it, and added nothing to the already existing powers of the United States.

The particular amendment now under consideration assumes the existence of the right of the people to assemble for lawful purposes, and protects it against encroachment by Congress. The right was not created by the amendment; neither was its continuance guaranteed, except as against congressional interference. For their protection in its enjoyment, therefore, the people must look to the States. The power for that purpose was originally placed there, and it has never been surrendered to the United States.

The right of the people peaceably to assemble for the purpose of petitioning Congress for a redress of grievances, or for any thing else connected with the powers or the duties of the national government, is an attribute of national citizenship, and, as such, under the protection of, and guaranteed by, the United States. The very idea of a government, republican in form, implies a right on the part of its citizens to meet peaceably for consultation in respect to public affairs and to petition for a redress of grievances. If it had been alleged in these counts that the object of the defendants was to prevent a meeting for such a purpose, the case would have been within the statute, and within the scope of the sovereignty of the United States. Such, however, is not the case. The offence, as stated in the indictment, will be made out, if it be shown that the object of the conspiracy was to prevent a meeting for any lawful purpose whatever....

The third and eleventh counts are even more objectionable. They charge the intent to have been to deprive the citizens named, they being in Louisiana, "of their respective several lives and liberty of person without due process of law." This is nothing else than alleging a conspiracy to falsely imprison or murder citizens of the United States, being within the territorial jurisdiction of the State of Louisiana. The rights of life and personal liberty are natural rights of man. "To secure these rights," says the Declaration of Independence, "governments are instituted among men, deriving their just powers from the consent of the governed." The very highest duty of the States, when they entered into the Union under the Constitution, was to protect all persons within their boundaries in the enjoyment of these "unalienable rights with which they were endowed by their Creator." Sovereignty, for this purpose, rests alone with the States. It is no more the duty or within the power of the United States to punish for a conspiracy to falsely imprison or murder within a State, than it would be to punish for false imprisonment or murder itself.

The fourteenth amendment prohibits a State from depriving any person of life, liberty, or property, without due process of law; but this adds nothing to the rights of one citizen as against another. It simply furnishes an additional guaranty against any encroachment by the States upon the fundamental rights which belong to every citizen as a member of society. As was said by Mr. Justice Johnson, in *Bank of Columbia v. Okely,* 4 Wheat. 244, it secures "the individual from the arbitrary exercise of the powers of government, unrestrained by the established principles of private rights and distributive justice." These counts in the indictment do not call for the exercise of any of the powers conferred by this provision in the amendment.

The fourth and twelfth counts charge the intent to have been to prevent and hinder the citizens named, who were of African descent and persons of color, in "the free exercise and enjoyment of their several rights and privileges to the full and equal benefit of all laws and proceedings, then and there, before that time, enacted or ordained by the said State of Louisiana and by the United States; and then and there, at that time, being in force in the said State and District of Louisiana aforesaid, for the security of their respective persons and property, then and there, at that time enjoyed at and within said State and District of Louisiana by white persons, being citizens of the said State of Louisiana and the United States, for the protection of the persons and property of said white citizens." There is no allegation that this was done because of the race or color of the persons conspired against. When stripped of its verbiage, the case as presented amounts to nothing more than that the defendants conspired to prevent certain citizens of the United States, being within the State of Louisiana, from enjoying the equal protection of the laws of the State and of the United States.

The fourteenth amendment prohibits a State from denying to any person within its jurisdiction the equal protection of the laws; but this provision does not, any more than the one which precedes it, and which we have just considered, add any thing to the rights which one citizen has under the Constitution against another. The equality of the rights of citizens is a principle of republicanism. Every republican government is duty bound to protect all its citizens in the enjoyment of this principle, if within its power. That duty was originally assumed by the States; and it still remains there. The only obligation resting upon the United States is to see that the States do not deny the right. This the amendment guarantees, but no more. The power of the national government is limited to the enforcement of this guaranty....

QUESTIONS

1.   According to the brief for the United States, why did the federal Government have the authority to enact legislation of the type at issue here?

2.   Does the decision reflect the federalism already discussed in Chapter 1 of the Essay? Do you find Waite's evidence convincing? Why or why not?

3.   Given the holding of this case, what relief was available in practical terms to those Southern blacks seeking protection from coercion and threats, if not actual harm?

Munn v. Illinois: *Lawyers' Briefs**

BRIEF FOR PLAINTIFFS IN ERROR—
JOHN N. JEWETT, ATTORNEY

...The right to the use and enjoyment of private property, the right to fix a value upon it, and upon its use by others, are parts of the very essence of private property. They are the elements which go to make up the very essence of private property, and without which the thing itself ceases to be either useful or desirable. A owns property, which he is using in the manner and for purposes wholly unobjectionable. It is neither injurious to the public health, nor to the public morals. It is not a nuisance, in any sense of that term. Legislation comes in, and says that B shall have the right to use that property, on specified conditions. B has no right to A's property, and therefore no right to be protected by such a law; and yet, A's property rights are invaded. Such a law, if law it could be called, would be in direct violation of the principle of protection to private property, and either the principle or the law must give way, because of this antagonism.

It is insisted that the Illinois Warehouse Law is of the latter class, in those particulars in which it is here objected to. It does not undertake to say that the warehouses, or the warehouse business, is a nuisance, nor in the objectionable sections does it pretend to regulate the manner in which the business shall be carried on. It even attempts, in some of its parts, to throw protection around the business, as though the public were desirous of its continuance in the usual way. It evidently contemplates its continuance, and its continuance is, in some sense, a public necessity; but while doing this, it strikes a blow, if it shall be sustained, with fearful certainty at the very foundation of private rights

* *Landmark Briefs and Arguments*, vol. 7, pp. 586–588.

in private property. It announces the doctrine that the public, or the legislature on behalf of the public, may usurp the private rights of the citizen, and take from him, one by one—or in the mass, it may be, all the elements which make up the idea of property; that he may be stripped of his property in the profitable use of his private estate; fixes a value upon the work of his own hands, and the product of his own brains, and says that at such a price, they may all be enjoyed by others, or that they shall not be enjoyed by him. This is destructive to property interests; it is destruction to all enterprise; it is death to the principle of protection to private rights. If the constitution cannot prevent this, it is a failure in one, at least, of its most essential purposes, and a legislative despotism is erected inside of institutions professedly republican. . . .

It has been said, that this section of the constitution was made solely for the benefit and protection of the Negro race, and the majority of the Supreme Court of Illinois seem to have imbibed that absurd idea. It cannot be so unless there is, in this country, one constitution for black people, and another for white, and that will not be contended. There is no objection to a reference to particular evils, prominently before the public mind, leading to the adoption of this article of the constitution, for the purpose of arriving at its proper interpretation. Indeed, I have, in this argument, endeavored to show that such a reference is legitimate, and in some cases necessary. But if I am not altogether mistaken in my apprehension of the force of language, a construction of this constitutional amendment, once arrived at, becomes universal in its application. The recently emancipated slaves were especially in a condition to need protection, in their civil and property rights, against invidious and discriminating State legislation. Their status, as citizens, was neither recognized, nor fixed by law, and the States in which they had resided as slaves, were scarcely willing, voluntarily, to elevate them to an equality of civil and political rights. This was the occasion for adopting [the fourteenth] amendment to the constitution; but the amendment, as adopted, embraces everybody. It is as broad as humanity, and the jurisdiction of the nation. Neither white men nor colored can monopolize its benefits, for it is without distinction of race or color, or previous condition of servitude. Admit that the condition of the colored race presented an illustration of the necessity for prohibiting State interference with individual rights, the prohibition once made, in terms of general import, becomes at once of universal application. It is by no means uncommon for a single case of hardship to suggest amendments to the law; but the law, when passed, unless limited by itself, applies not only to the special case which suggested it, but to all cases of a similar character. There can be no reasonable doubt, or argument contrary to this.

BRIEF FOR REHEARING—JOHN N. JEWETT, ATTORNEY FOR PLAINTIFFS IN ERROR*

It is not uncommon for the Supreme Court to receive requests for a rehearing, especially in a "major" case, as Jewett claimed this was. It is very uncommon, however, for the Court to grant a rehearing, and Munn v. Illinois *was no exception.*

The prominent position given by your Honors to this cause in the decision of a series of cases, involving to the last degree the existence of private rights in and over the wealth and industry of the country, whenever they come in contact with a public use or convenience, was as unexpected as it was unsought for by the plaintiffs in error and their counsel. The result of that position is to place before the world the case of Munn & Scott v. The People, etc., as an exponent of the estimation in which the judicial department of this government holds private interests, and the right of personal control over individual enterprises, and of the force and effect accorded by the same high authority to constitutional limitations upon the legislative power of the States. These are questions of immeasurable importance, not only to the millions of capital already invested in enterprises of a public, or quasi public character, and in the successful accomplishment of which the public have been largely, although indirectly interested; but also to the almost infinite variety of prospective improvements which are likely to present themselves in the progress of a still undeveloped territory, which experience has shown cannot be safely or economically undertaken by the States themselves, in their corporate capacity, and in the promotion of which it is against the expressed policy of the State, in a large majority of cases, to interfere. The case is thus made to assume an importance altogether disproportionate to the pecuniary interests directly involved in it. It reaches out to, and its decision is made to include the safety and stability of interests embracing a very large part of the invested private capital of the country, and must be looked to as the decisive exposition of the degree of protection which the constitution affords to private industry, energy and ability, and to the results which may be accomplished through their instrumentality.

* *Landmark Briefs and Arguments,* vol 7, pp. 661–663, 664–666.

It is not too much to say that the opinion of the Court in this case has sent a chill of apprehension through the very heart of the business enterprises of the nation, and that there is no interest or employment, however remotely connected with the public advantage, which does not sympathize with this apprehension. It has opened a new gateway of attack upon private industry, whenever its influence extends beyond the individual good, and concerns itself with the common welfare: it has pushed aside the obstructions which stood in the way of communism, or, at least, or the communistic spirit, against which the prohibitions of the constitution were directed. It has placed minorities in civil society at the very feet of political majorities, and rendered possible and probable even, the despotism of a political majority, which, if the constitution does not prevent, it but inaugurates the skeleton of a government, with vital forces only for evil; it makes the individual and his substance the legitimate prey for the body politic, and starts the government of the States on a new departure, the highway to the plundering of individual wealth, and the destruction of private enterprise.

The right of the State to take private property for public use, upon making just compensation therefore, has been well understood by all the people of this nation. They have been long familiar with the proposition that they held their property, subject to this ultimate right of the Government. They have recognized the fact, that public necessities might arise which would require of them a surrender of their personal possessions, however hallowed by private preferences or ancestral recollections; and when such necessities have arisen, they have acquiesced and yielded up their preferences and their wishes to the stern commands of a public law, which entertains as little respect for the graves of the dead and the memories of the living, as it does for the wild flowers which flourish and fade on the surface of the unbroken wilderness. But in doing this they have trusted to what was regarded as a principle of financial honesty, permeating and underlying the government of the State, engrafted into the constitution and rendered immutable by adoption as a maxim and axiom of State and Federal polity, that no citizen should be condemned without having an opportunity to be heard in his own defense, and that no man should be deprived of life, liberty or property without due process of law....

It is confidently submitted, that the conviction above mentioned, as to the sacredness of private property and private rights in private property, represents fairly the business and professional judgment of this country, as it has existed for the past one hundred years. If this was a mistaken judgment, the mistake has been a fatal one to many a private fortune, and it may prove equally fatal to the public, that the mistake has been discovered; but, in the confident belief that this judgment was sound in principle, just in theory, and well supported by consitutional guaranties, properly construed, and that the opinion of the Court in this cause is founded, to some extent, at least, upon a misapprehension of the facts of the case, a misapplication of the doctrines of the common law, and its maxims, and a construction of the constitutional guaranties to private rights, in a great degree subversive of the beneficial purposes they were intended to accomplish, the plaintiffs in error respectfully petition for a reconsideration of said opinion, and for a rehearing in said cause, and, in support of their petition, submit the following reasons and considerations:

I

The legislation under review in this case, whatever may be its pretensions, is aimed directly and solely at the warehouses and warehousemen of the city of Chicago. No persons or locations are mentioned in the act, which is limited, by its terms, to cities having 100,000 inhabitants and upwards. As there was no other city in Illinois, at the time of the passage of the act, having a population of one-fourth that number, it is quite superfluous to speak of the act as applying to "warehouses" at Chicago, and other places in the States having not less than "one hundred thousand inhabitants." It does not appear that the Court regarded it as of any importance whether the act had reference to the whole State, and to all warehouses and warehousemen within its jurisdiction, or to only a limited section of the territory of the State, and the warehouses located therein, although it was urged in the printed arguments, and some authorities were cited upon the point, that this local and discriminating feature of the act deprived it of the essential characteristics of a law, and reduced it to the proportions and qualities of individuals such as the courts have heretofore, pronounced to be without the legislative power, and therefore unconstitutional and void. It was, and still is, insisted, that such discriminating and personal legislation is repugnant to the last clause of the fourteenth amendment to the Constitution of the United States, which provides that no State shall "deny to any person within its jurisdiction the equal protection of the laws."

II

The old and trite formula, so often repeated, and so often made the pretext for pushing aside a constitutional question, that "every statute is presumed to be constitutional," is entitled to all the consideration which a formulated apology for hasty and passionate legislation can lay claim to. There is no reason, in fact, why a claim based upon a statute, should have any presumptions in its favor when that claim is made in the due course of judicial inquiry. In all cases, there should be a suspension of judicial judgment, until a clear apprehension of all the facts is arrived at, and it is clearly understood what the cause of complaint is, and how the elements of which it is composed arrange themselves with reference to constitutional provisions. If a State legislature should pass an act condemning a citizen to be burned at the stake, there is no apparent reason why it should have any presumption of constitutionality in its favor. The case may be an extreme one; but theories, to be reasonable, must be reasonable in their extremest application and consequences. It is not expected that there should be any presumption against the constitutionality of an act of a State legislature; but when a question of constitutionality is raised in the courts, it should stand, as any other question, unembarrassed by presumptions, and no weight or concurrence of authority can establish a reasonable formula to the contrary.

Munn v. Illinois*

JUSTICE FIELD, DISSENTING

I am compelled to dissent from the decision of the court in this case, and from the reasons upon which that decision is founded. The principle upon which the opinion of the majority proceeds is, in my judgment, subversive of the rights of private property, heretofore believed to be protected by constitutional guaranties against legislative interference, and is in conflict with the authorities cited in its support....

The doctrine of the State court, that no one is deprived of his property, within the meaning of the constitutional inhibition, so long as

*94 U.S. 113, 136, 141–142, 148, 152 (1877).

he retains its title and possession, and the doctrine of this court, that, whenever one's property is used in such a manner as to affect the community at large, it becomes by that fact clothed with a public interest, and ceases to be juris privati only, appear to me to destroy, for all useful purposes, the efficacy of the constitutional guaranty. All that is beneficial in property arises from its use, and the fruits of that use; and whatever deprives a person of them deprives him of all that is desirable or valuable in the title and possession. If the constitutional guaranty extends no further than to prevent a deprivation of title and possession, and allows a deprivation of use, and the fruits of that use, it does not merit the encomiums it has received. Unless I have misread the history of the provision now incorporated into all our State constitutions, and by the Fifth and Fourteenth Amendments into our Federal Constitution, and have misunderstood the interpretation it has received, it is not thus limited in its scope, and thus impotent for good. It has a much more extended operation than either court, State, or Federal has given to it. The provision, it is to be observed, places property under the same protection as life and liberty. Except by due process of law, no State can deprive any person of either. The provision has been supposed to secure to every individual the essential conditions for the pursuit of happiness; and for that reason has not been heretofore, and should never be, construed in any narrow or restricted sense.

No State "shall deprive any person of life, liberty or property without due process of law," says the Fourteenth Amendment to the Constitution. By the term "life," as here used, something more is meant than mere animal existence. The inhibition against its deprivation extends to all those limbs and faculties by which life is enjoyed. The provision equally prohibits the mutilation of the body by the amputation of an arm or leg, or the putting out of an eye, or the destruction of any other organ of the body through which the soul communicates with the outer world. The deprivation not only of life, but of whatever God has given to every one with life, for its growth and enjoyment, is prohibited by the provision in question, if its efficacy be not frittered away by judicial decision.

By the term "liberty," as used in the provision, something more is meant than mere freedom from physical restraint or the bounds of a prison. It means freedom to go where one may choose, and to act in such manner, not inconsistent with the equal rights of others, as his judgment may dictate for the promotion of his happiness; that is, to pursue such callings and avocations as may be most suitable to develop his capacities, and give to them their highest enjoyment.

The same liberal construction which is required for the protection of life and liberty, in all particulars in which life and liberty are of any value, should be applied to the protection of private property. If the legislature of a State, under pretence of providing for the public good, or for any other reason, can determine, against the consent of the owner, the uses to which private property shall be devoted, or the prices which the owner shall receive for its uses, it can deprive him of the property as completely as by a special act for its confiscation or destruction. . . .

There is nothing in the character of the business of the defendants as warehousemen which called for the interference complained of in this case. Their buildings are not nuisances; their occupation of receiving and storing grain infringes upon no rights of others, disturbs no neighborhood, infects not the air, and in no respect prevents others from using and enjoying their property as to them may seem best. The legislation in question is nothing less than a bold assertion of absolute power by the State to control at its discretion the property and business of the citizen, and fix the compensation he shall receive. The will of the legislature is made the condition upon which the owner shall receive the fruits of his property and the just reward of his labor, industry, and enterprise. . . .

But I deny the power of any legislature under our government to fix the price which one shall receive for his property of any kind. If the power can be exercised as to one article, it may as to all articles, and the prices of every thing, from a calico gown to a city mansion, may be the subject of legislative direction.

QUESTIONS

1. What evidence does Jewett offer for his claim that private property is protected by the Fourteenth Amendment? From what you have learned concerning the intentions of the framers, do you find his points convincing?

2. Jewett was well aware that the Supreme Court rarely declares acts of Congress unconstitutional. And he knew that striking down a state statute was also a step to be taken neither lightly nor frequently. How then can you explain Jewett's elaborate theory of judicial review, which emerges from his briefs in *Munn*? What were some of the conditions in America during the late nineteenth century that made such a theory appealing?

3. Note the tone of Jewett's brief for a rehearing. It is somewhat unusual for a lawyer to be so blunt in criticizing a decision handed down

by the very justices he is now petitioning for a rehearing. Why does Jewett feel that *Munn* "has sent a chill of apprehension through the very heart" of the business community?

4.   An important doctrine in American law is called the "presumption of constitutionality." It assumes that unless the evidence is overwhelmingly clear against the statute, it should be upheld—even if the judges have doubts concerning its utility or constitutionality. After all, it is the elected legislature, as representatives of the people, who enact statutes, not judges. Respect for the legislature therefore, requires the courts to affirm legislation unless it be "flagrantly wrong." According to Jewett, does the statute involved in *Munn* represent such a case? Why?

5.   Does Justice Field offer any evidence to support his "interpretation" of the Fourteenth Amendment? If not, on what does he build his argument?

IV.

Railroad Commissions

Massachusetts Railroad Commission Statute (1869) *

An Act to Establish a Board of Railroad Commissioners.

... The Governor, with the advice and consent of the Council, shall ... appoint three competent persons, who shall constitute a board of railroad commissioners, and who shall hold their offices from the dates of their respective appointments, for the term of one, two and three years, respectively, from the first day of July next. The governor shall, in like manner, before the first day of July in each year, appoint a commissioner, to continue in office for the term of three years from said day, and in case of any vacancy occurring in the board by resignation or otherwise, shall in the same manner appoint a commissioner for the residue of the term, and may in the same manner remove any commissioner.

* *Massachusetts Statutes, 1869,* Chapter 408, pp. 699–703.

Section 2. Said commissioners shall have the general supervision of all railroads in the Commonwealth, whether operated by steam, horse, or other motive power, and shall examine the same, and keep themselves informed as to their condition and the manner in which they are operated, with reference to the security and accommodation of the public, and the compliance of the several railroad corporations with the provisions of their charters and the laws of the Commonwealth.

Section 3. Whenever, in the judgment of the railroad commissioners, it shall appear that any railroad corporation fails, in any respect or particular, to comply with the terms of its charter or the laws of the Commonwealth; or whenever in their judgment any repairs are necessary upon its road, or any addition to its rolling stock, or any addition to or change of its stations or station-houses, or any change in its rates of fares for transporting freight or passengers, or any change in the mode of operating its road and conducting its business, is reasonable and expedient in order to promote the security, convenience and accommodation of the public, said railroad commissioners shall inform such railroad corporation of the improvements and changes, which they adjudge to be proper, by a notice thereof in writing, to be served by leaving a copy thereof, certified by the commissioners' clerk, with the clerk, treasurer or any director of said corporation; and a report of the proceedings shall be included in the annual report of the commissioners to the legislature.

Section 4. It shall be the duty of said commissioners upon the complaint and application of the mayor and alderman of any city, or the selectmen of any town, to make an examination of the condition and operation of any railroad, any part of whose location lies within the limit of such city or town; and if twenty or more legal voters in any city or town shall, by petition in writing, request the mayor and aldermen of such city, or the selectmen of such town, to make the said complaint and application, and the mayor and aldermen, or the selectmen, refuse or decline to comply with the prayer of the petition, they shall state the reason for such non-compliance in writing upon the petition, and return the same to the petitioners; and the petitioners may thereupon, with ten days from the date of such refusal and return, present said petition to said commissioners; and said commissioners shall, if upon due inquiry and hearing of the petitioners they think the public good demands the examination, proceed to make it in the same manner as if called upon by the mayor and aldermen of any city, or the selectmen of any town. Before proceeding to make such examination in accordance with such application or petition, said commissioners shall give to the petitioners and the corporation reasonable notice in writing of the time and place of entering upon the same. If upon such examination it shall appear to said commissioners that the complaint alleged by the applicants or petitioners is well founded, they shall so adjudge, and shall inform the corporation operating such railroad of their adjudication, in the same manner as is provided in the third section of this act....

Section 6. The several railroad corporations operating railroads within the Commonwealth, shall at all times on demand, furnish said commissioners any information required by them concerning the condition, management and operation of the railroads under their direction and control, respectively, and particularly with copies of all leases, contracts and agreements for transportation with express companies or otherwise, to which they are parties, and also with the rates for transporting freight and passengers upon their railroads, and upon the railroads with which their railroads respectively have connection in business.

Section 7. Said commissioners shall be provided with an office in the state house, or in some other suitable place in the city of Boston, in which their records shall be kept. In the discharge of the duties of their office, they shall be transported over the several railroads in the Commonwealth, free of charge; they may employ and take with them experts, or other agents, whose services they may deem to be temporarily of importance; they shall have a clerk, to be appointed by the governor, who shall receive a salary of two thousand dollars per annum, payable quarterly out of the treasury of the Commonwealth, and whose duty it shall be to keep a full and faithful record of the proceedings of said board of commissioners, and to serve such notices as may be required of him by the commissioners; and they may draw upon the treasurer of the Commonwealth for a sum not exceeding five hundred dollars annually, to be expended by them in procuring necessary books, maps, statistics, and stationary, and in defraying expenses incidental and necessary to the discharge of the duties of their office. A statement of such expenditures shall accompany their annual report.

Section 8. The annual salary of said commissioners shall be four thousand dollars each, payable quarterly from the treasury of the Commonwealth.

Section 9. The annual expenses of said board of commissioners, including salaries, shall be borne by the several corporations owning or operating the railroads in this Commonwealth in proportion to the income and profits of said corporations, for the year next preceding that in which the assessment hereinafter mentioned is made. And the tax commissioner shall, on or before the first day of July in each year, assess upon said corporations their just proportion of such expenses, which shall be collected from said corporations in the same manner as is provided by law for the collection of taxes upon corporations. . . .

Minnesota Railroad Commission Statute (1887)*

An Act to Regulate Common Carriers, and Creating the Railroad and Warehouse Commission of the State of Minnesota, . . .

Sec. 8. . . . (e) That in case the commission shall at any time find that any part of the tariffs of rates, fares, charges or classifications so filed and published as hereinbefore provided, are in any respect unequal or unreasonable, it shall have the power and is hereby authorized and directed to compel any common carrier to change the same and adopt such rate, fare, charge or classification as said commission shall declare to be equal and reasonable. To which end the commission shall, in writing, inform such common carrier, in what respect such tariffs shall be substituted therefor.

(f) In case such common carrier shall neglect or refuse for ten (10) days after such notice to substitute such tariff of rates, fares, charges or classifications, or to adopt the same as recommended by the commission, it shall be the duty of said commission to immediately publish such tariff of rates, fares, charges or classifications as they had declared to be equal and reasonable, and cause the same to be posted at all the regular stations on the line of such common carrier in this State, and thereafter it shall be unlawful for such common carrier to charge or maintain a higher or lower rate, fare, charge, or classification than that so fixed and published by said commission.

(g) If any common carrier, subject to the provisions of this act, shall neglect or refuse to publish or file its schedule of classifications, rates, fares or charges or any part thereof as provided in this section, or if any common carrier shall refuse or neglect to carry out such recommendations made and published by such commission, such common carrier shall be subject to a writ of mandamus, to be issued by any judge of the

Statute taken from 134 U.S. 422–427.

Supreme Court, or any of the district courts of this State upon application of the commission, to compel compliance with the requirements of this section and with the recommendation of the commission and failure to comply with the requirements of said writ of mandamus shall be punishable as and for contempt, and the said commission, as complainants, may also apply to any such judge for a writ of injunction against such common carrier from receiving or transporting property or passengers within this State until such common carrier shall have complied with the requirements of this section and the recommendation of said commission; and for any wilful violation or failure to comply with such requirements or such recommendation of said commission, the court may award such costs, including counsel fees, by way of penalty, on the return of said writs and after due deliberation thereon, as may be just.

Sec. 9. (a) That a commission is hereby created and established, to be known as the "Railroad and Warehouse Commission of the State of Minnesota," which shall be composed of three (3) commissioners, who shall be appointed by the governor, by and with the advice and consent of the senate....

Sec. 10. (a) That the commission hereby created shall have authority to enquire into the management of the business of all common carriers, subject to the provisions of this act, and shall keep itself informed as to the manner and method in which the same is conducted, and shall have the right to obtain from such common carriers full and complete information, necessary to enable the commission to perform the duties and carry out the objects for which it was created; in order to enable said commissioners efficiently to perform their duties under this act, it is hereby made their duty to cause one of their number to visit the various stations on the lines of each railroad as often as practicable, after giving twenty (20) days' notice of such visit and the time and place thereof in the local newspapers, and at least once in twelve (12) months to visit each county in the State in which is or shall be located a railroad station, and personally enquire into the management of small railroad business, and for this purpose, all railroad companies and common carriers, and their officers and employees, are required to aid and furnish each member of the railroad and warehouse commission with reasonable and proper facilities, and each, or all of the members of said commission, shall have the right, in his or their official capacity, to pass free on any railroad trains on all railroads in this State, and to enter and remain in at all suitable times, any and all cars, offices of depots, or upon the railroads of any railroad company in this State in the performance of official duties; and whenever, in the judgment of the commission, it shall appear that any common carrier fails in any respect or particular to comply with the laws of this State, or whenever in their judgment, any repairs are necessary upon its railroad, or any addition to or change of its stations or station-houses is necessary, or any change in the mode of operating its road or conducting its business is reasonable or expedient in order to promote the security, convenience and accommodation of the public, said commission shall inform such railroad company, by a notice thereof in writing, to be served as a summons in civil actions is required to be served by the statutes of this State in actions against corporations, certified by the commission's clerk or secretary, and if such common carrier shall neglect or refuse to comply with such order, then the commission may, in its discretion, cause suits or proceedings to be instituted to enforce its orders as provided in this act.

Sec. 11. That in case any common carrier, subject to the provisions of this act, shall do, cause to be done, or permit to be done, any act or thing in this act prohibited or declared to be unlawful, or shall omit to do any act, matter or thing in this act required to be done, such common carrier shall be liable to the person or persons, party or parties injured thereby, for the full amount of damages sustained in consequence of any such violation of the provisions of this act, together with a reasonable counsel or attorney's fees shall be taxed and collected as part of the costs in the case.

QUESTIONS

1. Compare the commissions established by the Massachusetts and Minnesota statutes. Note that they represent two very different models for administrative regulation. What are the basic similarities and differences?

2. Do the two statutes reflect differing philosophies toward state regulation? Which one appears more powerful? Why?

3. Who provides the money, under the Massachusetts statute, to pay the salaries and expenses of the commissioners? Why might the answer to this question be an important issue in state regulation?

The Minnesota Rate Case*

JUSTICE BLATCHFORD: OPINION OF THE COURT

The construction put upon the statute by the Supreme Court of Minnesota must be accepted by this court, for the purpose of the present case, as conclusive and not to be reexamined here as to its propriety or accuracy. The Supreme Court authoritatively declares that it is the expressed intention of the legislature of Minnesota, by the statute, that the rates recommended and published by the commission, if it proceeds in the manner pointed out by the act, are not simply advisory, nor merely prima facie equal and reasonable, but final and conclusive as to what are equal and reasonable charges; that the law neither contemplates nor allows any issue to be made or inquiry to be had as to their equality or reasonableness in fact; that, under the statute, the rates published by the commission are the only ones that are lawful, and, therefore, in contemplation of law the only ones that are equal and reasonable; and that, in a proceeding for a mandamus under the statute, there is no fact to traverse except the violation of law in not complying with the recommendations of the commission. In other words, although the railroad company is forbidden to establish rates that are not equal and reasonable, there is no power in the courts to stay the hands of the commission, if it chooses to establish rates that are unequal and unreasonable.

This being the construction of the statute by which we are bound in considering the present case, we are of opinion that, so construed, it conflicts with the Constitution of the United States in the particulars complained of by the railroad company. It deprives the company of its right to a judicial investigation, by due process of law, under the forms and with the machinery provided by the wisdom of successive ages for the investigation judicially of the truth of a matter in controversy, and substitutes therefor, as an absolute finality, the action of a railroad commission which, in view of the powers conceded to it by the state court, cannot be regarded as clothed with judicial functions or possessing the machinery of a court of justice.

Under section 8 of the statute, which the Supreme Court of Minnesota says is the only one which relates to the matter of the fixing

---

* *Chicago, Milwaukee and St. Paul Railway Co., v. Minnesota,* 134 U.S. 418, 456-459 (1890).

by the commission of general schedules of rates, and which section, it says, fully and exclusively provides for that subject, and is complete in itself, all that the commission is required to do is, on the filing with it by a railroad company of copies of its schedules of charges, to "find" that any part thereof is in any respect unequal or unreasonable, and then it is authorized and directed to compel the company to change the same and adopt such charge as the commission "shall declare to be equal and reasonable," and, to that end, it is required to inform the company in writing in what respect its charges are unequal and unreasonable. No hearing is provided for, no summons or notice to the company before the commission has found what it is to find and declared what it is to declare, no opportunity provided for the company to introduce witnesses before the commission, in fact, nothing which has the semblance of due process of law; and although, in the present case, it appears that, prior to the decision of the commission, the company appeared before it by its agent, and the commission investigated the rates charged by the company for transporting milk, yet it does not appear what the character of the investigation was or how the result was arrived at.

By the second section of the statute in question, it is provided that all charges made by a common carrier for the transportation of passengers or property shall be equal and reasonable. Under this provision, the carrier has a right to make equal and reasonable charges for such transportation. In the present case, the return alleged that the rate of charge fixed by the commission was not equal or reasonable, and the Supreme Court held that the statute deprived the company of the right to show that judicially. The question of the reasonableness of a rate of charge for transportation by a railroad company, involving as it does the element of reasonableness both as regards the company and as regards the public, is eminently a question for judicial investigation, requiring due process of law for its determination. If the company is deprived of the power of charging reasonable rates for the use of its property, and such deprivation takes place in the absence of an investigation by judicial machinery, it is deprived of the lawful use of its property, and thus, in substance and effect, of the property itself, without due process of law and in violation of the Constitution of the United States; and in so far as it is thus deprived, while other persons are permitted to receive reasonable profits upon their invested capital, the company is deprived of the equal protection of the laws....

The issuing of the peremptory writ of mandamus in this case was, therefore, unlawful, because in violation of the Constitution of the United States; and it is necessary that the relief administered in favor of the plaintiff in error should be a reversal of the judgment of the Supreme Court awarding that writ, and an instruction for further proceedings by it not inconsistent with the opinion of this court.

In view of the opinion delivered by that court, it may be impossible for any further proceedings to be taken other than to dismiss the proceeding for a mandamus, if the court should adhere to its opinion that, under the statute, it cannot investigate judicially the reasonableness of the rates fixed by the commission. Still, the question will be open for review; and

The judgment of this court is, that the judgment of the Supreme Court of Minnesota, entered May 4, 1888, awarding a peremptory writ of mandamus in this case, be reversed....

JUSTICE BRADLEY, DISSENTING*

I cannot agree to the decision of the court in this case. It practically overrules Munn v. Illinois, 94 U.S. 113, and the several railroad cases that were decided at the same time. The governing principle of those cases was that the regulation and settlement of the fares of railroads and other public accommodations is a legislative prerogative and not a judicial one. This is a principle which I regard as of great importance. When a railroad company is chartered, it is for the purpose of performing a duty which belongs to the State itself. It is chartered as an agent of the State for furnishing public accommodation. The State might build its railroads if it saw fit. It is its duty and its prerogative to provide means of intercommunication between one part of its territory and another. If the legislature commissions private parties, whether corporations or individuals, to perform this duty, it is its prerogative to fix the fares and freights which they may charge for their services. When merely a road or a canal is to be constructed, it is for the legislature to fix the tolls to be paid by those who use it; when a company is chartered not only to build a road, but to carry on public transportation upon it, it is for the legislature to fix the charges for such transportation.

But it is said that all charges should be reasonable, and that none but reasonable charges can be exacted; and it is urged that what is a reasonable charge is a judicial question. On the contrary, it is

* Justices Gray and Lamar concurred with this dissent. 134 U.S. 418, 461–464, 465–466 (1890).

preeminently a legislative one, involving considerations of policy as well as of remuneration; and is usually determined by the legislature, by fixing a maximum of charges in the charter of the company, or afterwards, if its hands are not tied by contract. If this maximum is not exceeded, the courts cannot interfere. When the rates are not thus determined, they are left to the discretion of the company, subject to the express or implied condition that they shall be reasonable; express, when so declared by statute; implied, by the common law, when the statute is silent; and the common law has effect by virtue of the legislative will.

Thus, the legislature either fixes the charges at rates which it deems reasonable; or merely declares that they shall be reasonable; and it is only in the latter case, where what is reasonable is left open, that the courts have jurisdiction of the subject. I repeat: When the legislature declares that the charges shall be reasonable, or, which is the same thing, allows the common law rule to that effect to prevail, and leaves the matter there; then resort may be had to the courts to inquire judicially whether the charges are reasonable. Then, and not till then, is it a judicial question. But the legislature has the right, and it is its prerogative, if it chooses to exercise it, to declare what is reasonable.

This is just where I differ from the majority of the court. They say in effect, if not in terms, that the final tribunal of arbitrament is the judiciary; I say it is the legislature. I hold that it is a legislative question, not a judicial one, unless the legislature or the law, (which is the same thing,) has made it judicial, by prescribing the rule that the charges shall be reasonable, and leaving it there.

It is always a delicate thing for the courts to make an issue with the legislative department of the government, and they should never do so if it is possible to avoid it. By the decision now made we declare, in effect, that the judiciary, and not the legislature, is the final arbiter in the regulation of fares and freights of railroads and the charges of other public accommodations. It is an assumption of authority on the part of the judiciary which, it seems to me, with all due deference to the judgment of my brethren, it has no right to make. The assertion of jurisdiction by this court makes it the duty of every court of general jurisdiction, state or federal, to entertain complaints against the decisions of the boards of commissioners appointed by the States to regulate their railroads; for all courts are bound by the Constitution of the United States, the same as we are. Our jurisdiction is merely appellate....

I think it is perfectly clear, and well settled by the decisions of this court, that the legislature might have fixed the rates in question. If it had done so, it would have done it through the aid of committees appointed to investigate the subject, to acquire information, to cite parties, to get all the facts before them, and finally to decide and report. No one could have said that this was not due process of law. And if the legislature itself could do this, acting by its committees, and proceeding according to the usual forms adopted by such bodies, I can see no good reason why it might not delegate the duty to a board of commissioners, charged, as the board in this case was, to regulate and fix the charges, so as to be equal and reasonable. Such a board would have at its command all the means of getting at the truth and ascertaining the reasonableness of fares and freights, which a legislative committee has. It might, or it might not, swear witnesses and examine parties. Its duties being of an administrative character, it would have the widest scope for examination and inquiry. All means of knowledge and information would be at its command,—just as they would be at the command of the legislature which created it. Such a body, though not a court, is a proper tribunal for the duties imposed upon it. . . .

It is complained that the decisions of the board are final and without appeal. So are the decisions of the courts in matters within their jurisdiction. There must be a final tribunal somewhere for deciding every question in the world. Injustice may take place in all tribunals. All human institutions are imperfect—courts as well as commissions and legislatures. Whatever tribunal has jurisdiction, its decisions are final and conclusive unless an appeal is given therefrom. The important question always is, what is the lawful tribunal for the particular case? In my judgment, in the present case, the proper tribunal was the legislature, or the board of commissioners which it created for the purpose. . . .

It may be that our legislatures are invested with too much power, open, as they are, to influences so dangerous to the interests of individuals, corporations and society. But such is the Constitution of our republican form of government; and we are bound to abide by it until it can be corrected in a legitimate way. If our legislatures become too arbitrary in the exercise of their powers, the people always have a remedy in their hands; they may at any time restrain them by constitutional limitations. But so long as they remain invested with the powers that ordinarily belong to the legislative branch of government, they are entitled to exercise those powers, amongst which, in my judgment, is that of the regulation of railroads and other public means of intercommunication, and the burdens and charges which those who own them are authorized to impose upon the public.

QUESTIONS

1. In what sense does the Court's decision represent a basic change in its philosophy since *Munn* in 1877?

2. How, according to the Court, does the Minnesota statute fail to provide due process for the railroads? (See paragraphs e, f, and g of section 8 in the Minnesota statute.)

3. Does the Court declare the statute unconstitutional? If not, what does it do?

4. Note that the majority opinion does not mention *Munn* at all. Is Justice Bradley correct when he states that the decision "practically overrules" the 1877 holding? Why or why not?

V.

Statutes of Incorporation

State of Illinois: Act for the Incorporation of Boards of Trade and Chambers of Commerce (1849)*

Section 1. Be it enacted by the People of the State of Illinois, represented in the General Assembly, That any number of persons not less than twenty, residing in any town or city, may associate themselves together as a Board of Trade, and assemble at any time and place upon which a majority of the members so associating themselves together may agree, and see fit, adopt a name, constitution and by-laws such as they may agree upon, and shall thereupon become a Body Corporate which they may have adopted, and by that name shall have succession, shall be capable in law to sue and be sued, plead and be impleaded, answer and be answered, defend and be defended, in all courts of law and equity whatever, and they and their successors shall have a common seal, and may alter and change the same at their discretion.

*Taken from pamphlet F38N6, B6a, 1850, Chicago Historical Society.

Sec. 2. Said corporation shall have the right to admit as members such persons as they may see fit, and expel any members as they may see fit; and in all cases a majority of the members present at any stated meetings shall have the right to pass, and also the right to repeal, any by-laws of said corporation; and in all cases the constitution and by-laws adopted by such corporation shall be binding upon and control the same until altered, changed or abrogated in the manner that may be prescribed in such constitution.

Sec. 3. Said corporation, by the name and style which shall be adopted, shall be capable in law of purchasing, holding and conveying any estate, real or personal, for the use of said corporation.

Provided, Such real estate shall not exceed in quantity one city, town or village lot, and building, in the city, town or village where said corporation may be located.

Sec. 4. The officers shall hold their offices for the time which shall be prescribed in the constitution adopted by such corporation, and until others shall be elected and qualified as prescribed by such constitution.

Sec. 5. The President, Vice President, Secretary and Treasurer, shall be, ex-officio, members of the Board of Directors, and together with the Directors elected, shall manage the business of said corporation.

Sec. 6. All officers shall be elected by a plurality of votes given at any election, and a general election of officers shall be held at least once in each year; but in case of any accident, failure or neglect, to hold such general election, the corporation shall not thereby lapse or terminate, but shall continue and exist, and the old officers shall hold over until the next general election of officers provided for in the constitution.

Sec. 7. The award of any general committee of reference appointed by said corporation, upon any matter of difference submitted to such committee for arbitration in writing, with or without seal, by any member of said corporation or by any other person whomsoever, shall have the same force and effect as if the same had been submitted to the arbitration of the members of said committee of reference by their individual names, by deed of submission, and such award may be filed and made a rule of court, and judgment entered thereon, and execution issued, in the same manner, and under the same rules and regulations that other awards may be entered, under and by virtue of the provisions of the seventh chapter of the revised statutes entitled "Arbitrations and Awards." Writs of error may be had, and appeals taken from the decision of the court, in the same manner as is prescribed in said chapter.

Sec. 8. No submission bond, or arbitration bond shall be required to be filed with such awards, but four days notice of the filing of such award shall be given to the opposite party of the party filing the award; said committee of reference, when sitting as arbitrators as aforesaid, shall have the right to issue subpoenas, and compel the attendance of witnesses by attachment, the same as Justices of the Peace.

Sec. 9. Said corporation may inflict fines upon any of its members, and collect the same for breach of the provisions of the constitution or by-laws—but no fine shall in any case exceed five dollars. Such fines may be collected by action of debt brought in the name of the corporation, before any Justice of the Peace, against the person upon whom the fine shall have been imposed.

Sec. 10. Said corporation shall have no power or authority to do or carry on any business, excepting such as is usual in the management of Boards of Trade, or Chambers of Commerce, and as provided for in the foregoing sections of this bill.

State of New Jersey: Act Concerning Corporations (1875)*

FORMATION, CONSTITUTION, ALTERATION, DISSOLUTION

10. It shall be lawful for any three or more persons to associate themselves into a company to carry on any kind of manufacturing, mining, chemical, trading or agricultural business, the transportation of goods, merchandise or passengers, upon land or water, inland navigation, the building of houses, vessels, wharves or docks, or other mechanical business, the reclamation and improvement of submerged lands, the improvement and sale of lands, the making, purchasing and selling [of] manufactured articles, and also of acquiring and disposing of rights to make and use the same, the renting of buildings and steam or other power therewith, the cutting and digging of peat, stone, marl, clay or other like substance, and dealing in the same, manufactured or unmanufactured, or any wholesale or retail mercantile business, or any lawful business or purpose whatever, upon making and filing a certificate in writing of their organization, in manner hereinafter mentioned; provided, that nothing herein contained shall be construed to authorize the formation of any railroad company, turnpike company

* *Revised Statutes of the State of New Jersey,* 1877, pp. 179–180.

or any other company which shall need to possess the right of taking and condemning lands, nor of any insurance company, banking company, savings bank, or other corporation intended to derive profit from the loan or use of money.

11. Such certificate in writing shall set forth—

I. The name assumed to designate such company, and to be used in its business and dealings;

II. The place or places in this state or elsewhere where the business of such company is to be conducted, and the objects for which the company shall be formed;

III. The total amount of the capital stock of such company, which shall not be less than two thousand dollars, the amount with which they will commence business, which shall not be less than one thousand dollars, and the number of shares into which the same is divided, and the par value of each share;

IV. The names and residences of the stockholders, and the number of shares held by each;

V. The periods at which such company shall commence and terminate, not exceeding fifty years;

Which certificates shall be proved or acknowledged and recorded, as required of deeds of real estate, in a book to be kept for that purpose in the office of the clerk of the county where the principal office or place of business of such company in this state shall be established, and, after being so recorded, shall be filed in the office of the secretary of state; the certificate may contain any limitation upon the powers of the corporation, the directors and the stockholders, that the parties signing the same desire; provided, such limitation does not attempt to exempt the corporation, the directors or the stockholders, from the performance of any duty imposed by law.

12. The said certificate, or a copy thereof, duly certified by said clerk or secretary, shall be evidence in all courts and places.

13. Upon making said certificate, and causing the same to be recorded and filed as aforesaid, the said persons so associating, their successors and assigns, shall be, from the time of commencement fixed in said certificate, and until the time limited therein for the termination thereof, incorporated into a company, by the name mentioned in said certificate; provided, that the legislature may, at pleasure, dissolve any company created by virtue of this act.

14. All companies that may be hereafter established within this state, under the provisions hereinabove contained, or under any law of this state, and also the officers of every such company, and the stockholders therein, may exercise the powers, and shall be governed by the provisions, and be subject to the liabilities hereinbefore and hereinafter provided.

15. Any company organized as aforesaid may carry on a part of its business out of this state, and have one or more offices and places of business out of this state, and may hold, purchase and convey real and personal property out of this state the same as if such real and personal property were situate in the state of New Jersey....

QUESTIONS

1. List some specific examples in the Illinois and New Jersey statutes that demonstrate the ease with which it became possible to incorporate?

2. Why might this point be considered important in explaining late-nineteenth-century economic development?

3. One of the goals of business associations during the late nineteenth century was to avoid, if at all possible, long, expensive court cases. How does the Illinois statute address this problem?

VI.

Restraint of Trade

*The Sherman Antitrust Act (1890)**

An act to protect trade and commerce against unlawful restraints and monopolies.

Be it enacted by the Senate and the House of Representatives of the United States of America in Congress assembled,

SECTION 1. Every contract, combination in the form of trust or othewise, or conspiracy, in restraint of trade or commerce among the several States, or with foreign nations, is hereby declared to be illegal. Every person who shall make any such contract or engage in any such

* 26 Stat., 209.

combination or conspiracy shall be deemed guilty of a misdemeanor, and, on conviction thereof, shall be punished by fine not exceeding five thousand dollars, or by imprisonment not exceeding one year, or by both said punishments, in the discretion of the court.

SECTION 2. Every person who shall monopolize, or attempt to monopolize, or combine or conspire with any other person or persons, to monopolize any part of the trade or commerce among the several States, or with foreign nations, shall be deemed guilty of a misdemeanor, and, on conviction thereof, shall be punished by fine not exceeding five thousand dollars, or by imprisonment not exceeding one year, or by both said punishments, in the discretion of the court.

SECTION 3. Every contract, combination in the form of trust or otherwise, or conspiracy, in restraint of trade or commerce in any Territory of the United States or of the District of Columbia, or in restraint of trade or commerce between any such Territory and another, and between any such Territory or Territories and any State or States or the District of Columbia, or with foreign nations, is hereby declared illegal. Every person who shall make any such contract or engage in any such combination or conspiracy shall be deemed guilty of a misdemeanor, and, on conviction thereof, shall be punished by fine not exceeding five thousand dollars, or by imprisonment not exceeding one year, or by both said punishments, in the discretion of the court.

SECTION 4. The several circuit courts of the United States are hereby invested with jurisdiction to prevent and restrain violations of this Act; and it shall be the duty of the several district attorneys of the United States, in their respective districts, under the direction of the Attorney General, to institute proceedings in equity to prevent and restrain such violations. Such proceedings may be by way of petition setting forth the case and praying that such violation shall be enjoined or otherwise prohibited. When the parties complained of shall have been duly notified of such petitions the court shall proceed, as soon as may be, to the hearing and determination of the case; and pending such petition and before final decree, the court may at any time make such temporary restraining order or prohibition as shall be deemed just in the premises.

United States v. E. C. Knight Co.*

CHIEF JUSTICE FULLER: OPINION OF THE COURT

The fundamental question is, whether conceding that the existence of a monopoly in manufacture is established by the evidence, that monopoly can be directly suppressed under the act of Congress in the mode attempted by this bill. . . .

The argument is that the power to control the manufacture of refined sugar is a monopoly over a necessary of life, to the enjoyment of which by a large part of the population of the United States interstate commerce is indispensable, and that, therefore, the general government in the exercise of the power to regulate commerce may repress such monopoly directly and set aside the instruments which have created it. But this argument cannot be confined to necessaries of life merely, and must include all articles of general consumption. Doubtless the power to control the manufacture of a given thing involves in a certain sense the control of its disposition, but this is a secondary and not the primary sense; and although the exercise of that power may result in bringing the operation of commerce into play, it does not control it, and affects it only incidentally and indirectly. Commerce succeeds to manufacture, and is not a part of it. The power to regulate commerce is the power to prescribe the rule by which commerce shall be governed, and is a power independent of the power to suppress monopoly. But it may operate in repression of monopoly whenever that comes within the rules by which commerce is governed or whenever the transaction is itself a monopoly of commerce.

It is vital that the independence of the commercial power and of the police power, and the delimitation between them, however sometimes perplexing, should always be recognized and observed, for while the one furnishes the strongest bond of union, the other is essential to the preservation of the autonomy of the States as required by our dual form of government; and acknowledged evils, however grave and urgent they may appear to be, had better be borne, than the risk be run, in the effort to suppress them, of more serious consequences by resort to expedients of even doubtful constitutionality.

It will be perceived how far-reaching the proposition is that the power of dealing with a monopoly directly may be exercised by the

* 156 U.S. 1, 11–13, 14–15 (1895).

general government whenever interstate or international commerce may be ultimately affected. The regulation of commerce applies to the subjects of commerce and not to matters of internal police. Contract to buy, sell, or exchange goods to be transported among the several States, the transportation and its instrumentalities, and articles bought, sold, or exchanged for the purposes of such transit among the States, or put in the way of transit, may be regulated, but this is because they form part of interstate trade or commerce. The fact that an article is manufactured for export to another States does not of itself make it an article of interstate commerce, and the intent of the manufacturer does not determine the time when the article or product passes from the control of the State and belongs to commerce....

Contracts, combinations, or conspiracies to control domestic enterprise in manufacture, agriculture, mining, production in all its forms, or to raise or lower prices or wages, might unquestionably tend to restrain external as well as domestic trade, but the restraint would be an indirect result, however inevitable and whatever its extent, and such result would not necessarily determine the object of the contract, combination, or conspiracy.

Again, all the authorities agree that in order to vitiate a contract or combination it is not essential that its result should be a complete monopoly; it is sufficient if it really tends to that end and to deprive the public of the advantages which flow from free competition. Slight reflection will show that if the national power extends to all contracts and combinations in manufacture, agriculture, mining and other productive industries, whose ultimate result may affect external commerce, comparatively little of business operations and affairs would be left for state control.

It was in the light of well-settled principles that the act of July 2, 1890, was framed. Congress did not attempt thereby to assert the power to deal with monopoly directly as such; or to limit and restrict the rights of corporations created by the States or the citizens of the States in the acquisition, control, or disposition of property; or to regulate or prescribe the price or prices at which such property or the products thereof should be sold; or to make criminal the acts of persons in the acquisition and control of property which the States of their residence or creation sanctioned or permitted. Aside from the provisions applicable where Congress might exercise municipal power, what the law struck at was combinations, contracts, and conspiracies to monopolize trade and commerce among the several States or with foreign nations; but the contracts and acts of the defendants related exclusively to the acquisition of the Philadelphia refineries and the business of sugar refining in Pennsylvania, and bore no direct relation to commerce between the States or with foreign nations. The object was manifestly private gain in the manufacture of the commodity, but not through the control of interstate or foreign commerce. It is true that the bill alleged that the products of these refineries were sold and distributed among the several States, and that all the companies were engaged in trade or commerce with the several States and with foreign nations; but this was no more than to say that trade and commerce served manufacture to fulfil its function. Sugar was refined for sale, and sales were probably made at Philadelphia for consumption, and undoubtedly for resale by the first purchasers throughout Pennsylvania and other States, and refined sugar was also forwarded by the companies to other States for sale. Nevertheless, it does not follow that an attempt to monopolize, or the actual monopoly of, the manufacture was an attempt, whether executory or consummated, to monopolize commerce, even though, in order to dispose of the product, the instrumentality of commerce was necessarily invoked....

JUSTICE HARLAN, DISSENTING*

If this combination, so far as its operations necessarily or directly affect interstate commerce, cannot be restrained or suppressed under some power granted to Congress, it will be cause for regret that the patriotic statesmen who framed the Constitution did not foresee the necessity of investing the national government with power to deal with gigantic monopolies holding in their grasp, and injuriously controlling in their own interest, the entire trade among the States in food products that are essential to the comfort of every household in the land....

The court holds it to be vital in our system of government to recognize and give effect to both the commercial power of the nation and the police powers of the States, to the end that the Union be strengthened and the autonomy of the States preserved. In this view I entirely concur. Undoubtedly, the preservation of the just authority of the States is an object of deep concern to every lover of his country. No greater calamity could befall our free institutions than the destruction of that authority, by whatever means such a result might be accomplished.

* 156 U.S. 1, 19, 42, 44–45 (1895).

"Without the States in union," this court has said, "there could be no such political body as the United States." *Lane County v. Oregon,* 7 Wall. 71, 76. But it is equally true that the preservation of the just authority of the General Government is essential as well to the safety of the States as to the attainment of the important ends for which that government was ordained by the People of the United States; and the destruction of that authority would be fatal to the peace and well-being of the American people. The Constitution which enumerates the powers committed to the nation for objects of interest to the people of all the States should not, therefore, be subjected to an interpretation so rigid, technical, and narrow, that those objects cannot be accomplished. . . .

While the opinion of the court in this case does not declare the act of 1890 to be unconstitutional, it defeats the main object for which it was passed. For it is, in effect, held that the statute would be unconstitutional if interpreted as embracing such unlawful restraints upon the purchasing of goods in one State to be carried to another State as necessarily arise from the *existence* of combinations formed for the purpose and with the effect, not only of monopolizing the ownership of all such goods in every part of the country, but of controlling the prices for them in all the States. This view of the scope of the act leaves the public, so far as national power is concerned, entirely at the mercy of combinations which arbitrarily control the prices of articles purchased to be transported from one State to another State. I cannot assent to that view. In my judgment, the general government is not placed by the Constitution in such a condition of helplessness that it must fold its arms and remain inactive while capital combines, under the name of the corporation, to destroy competition, not in one State only, but throughout the entire country, in the buying and selling of articles— especially the necessaries of life—that go into commerce among the States. The doctrine of the autonomy of the States cannot properly be invoked to justify a denial of power in the national government to meet such an emergency, involving as it does that freedom of commercial intercourse among the States which the Constitution sought to attain. . . .

We have before us the case of a combination which absolutely controls, or may, at its discretion, control the price of all refined sugar in this country. Suppose another combination, organized for private gain and to control prices, should obtain possession of all the large flour mills in the United States; another, of all the grain elevators; another, of all the oil territory; another, of all the salt-producing regions; another, of all the cotton mills; and another, of all the great establishments for slaughtering animals, and the preparation of meats. What power is competent to protect the people of the United States against such dangers except a national power—one that is capable of exerting its sovereign authority throughout every part of the territory and over all the people of the nation?

To the general government has been committed the control of commercial intercourse among the States, to the end that it may be free at all times from any restraints except such as Congress may impose or permit for the benefit of the whole country. The common government of all the people is the only one that can adequately deal with a matter which directly and injuriously affects the entire commerce of the country, which concerns equally all the people of the Union, and which, it must be confessed, cannot be adequately controlled by any one State. Its authority should not be so weakened by construction that it cannot reach and eradicate evils that, beyond all question, tend to defeat an object which that government is entitled, by the Constitution, to accomplish. "Powerful and ingenious minds," this court has said, "taking, as postulates, that the powers expressly granted to the government of the Union, are to be contracted by construction into the narrowest possible compass, and that the original powers of the States are retained if any possible construction will retain them, may by a course of well digested, but refined metaphysical reasoning, founded on these premises, explain away the Constitution of our country, and leave it, a magnificent structure, indeed, to look at, but totally unfit for use. They may so entangle and perplex the understanding as to obscure principles which were before thought quite plain, and induce doubts where, if the mind were to pursue its own course, none would be perceived." *Gibbons v. Ogden,* 9 Wheat. 1, 222 (1824)

QUESTIONS

1. Is the Sherman Act narrow or broad in scope? Exactly what is forbidden under it? What does it say about competition?

2. Because the government in making its case did not discuss the relationship of the sugar trust's manufacturing arrangements to interstate commerce, the Court declined to consider this point. Did this exercise of "judicial restraint" distort the intentions of the Sherman Act?

3. Is Justice Harlan correct when he claims that the majority opinion "defeats the main object" of the statute? In the last paragraph of his dissent, what does he accuse the majority of doing? Is his accusation justified?

Northern Securities Co. v. United States*

JUSTICE HOLMES, DISSENTING

I am unable to agree with the judgment of the majority of the court, and although I think it useless and undesirable, as a rule, to express dissent, I feel bound to do so in this case and to give my reasons for it.

Great cases like hard cases make bad law. For great cases are called great, not by reason of their real importance in shaping the law of the future, but because of some accident of immediate overwhelming interest which appeals to the feelings and distorts the judgment. These immediate interests exercise a kind of hydraulic pressure which makes what previously was clear seem doubtful, and before which even well settled principles of law will bend. What we have to do in this case is to find the meaning of some not very difficult words. We must try, I have tried, to do it with the same freedom of natural and spontaneous interpretation that one would be sure of if the same question arose upon an indictment for a similar act which excited no public attention, and was of importance only to a prisoner before the court. Furthermore, while at times judges need for their work the training of economists or statesmen, and must act in view of their foresight of consequences, yet when their task is to interpret and apply the words of a statute, their function is merely academic to begin with—to read English intelligently—and a consideration of consequences comes into play, if at all, only when the meaning of the words used is open to reasonable doubt.

The question to be decided is whether, under the act of July 2, 1890, c 647, 26 Stat. 209, it is unlawful, at any stage of the process, if several men unite to form a corporation for the purpose of buying more than half the stock of each of two competing interstate railroad companies, if they form the corporation, and the corporation buys the stock. I will suppose further that every step is taken, from the beginning, with the single intent of ending competition between the companies. I make this addition not because, it may not be and is not disputed but because, as I shall try to show, it is totally unimportant under any part of the statute with which we have to deal.

The statute of which we have to find the meaning is a criminal statute. The two sections on which the Government relies both make certain acts crimes. That is their immediate purpose and that is what they say. It is vain to insist that this is not a criminal proceeding. The words cannot be read one way in a suit which is to end in fine and imprisonment and another way in one which seeks an injunction. The construction which is adopted in this case must be adopted in one of the other sort. I am no friend of artificial interpretations because a statute is of one kind rather than another, but all agree that before a statute is to be taken to punish that which always has been lawful it must express its intent in clear words. So I say we must read the words before us as if the question were whether two small exporting grocers should go to jail.

Again the statute is of a very sweeping and general character. It hits "every" contract or combination of the prohibited sort, great or small, and "every" person who shall monopolize or attempt to monopolize, in the sense of the act, "any part" of the trade or commerce among the several States. There is a natural inclination to assume that it was directed against certain great combinations and to read it in that light. It does not say so. On the contrary, it says "every," and "any part." Still less was it directed specially against railroads. There even was a reasonable doubt whether it included railroads until the point was decided by this court. . . .

The first section makes "Every contract, combination in the form of trust or otherwise, or conspiracy in restraint of trade or commerce among the several States, or with foreign nations" a misdemeanor, punishable by fine, imprisonment or both. Much trouble is made by substituting other phrases assumed to be equivalent, which then are reasoned from as if they were in the act. The court below argued as if maintaining competition were the expressed object of the act. The act says nothing about competition. I stick to the exact words used. The words hit two classes of cases, and only two—Contracts in restraint of trade and combinations or conspiracies in restraint of trade, and we have to consider what these respectively are. . . .

What I now ask is under which of the foregoing classes this case is supposed to come, and that question must be answered as definitely and precisely as if we were dealing with the indictments which logically ought to follow this decision. The provision of the statute against contracts in restraint of trade has been held to apply to contracts between railroads, otherwise remaining independent, by which they restricted their respective freedom as to rates. This restriction by contract with a stranger to the contractor's business is the ground of the decision in *United States v. Joint Traffic Association,* 171 U.S. 505, following and affirming *United States v. Trans-Missouri Freight Association,* 166 U.S. 290. I accept those decisions absolutely, not only as binding upon me, but as decisions which I have no desire to criticise or abridge. But the provision has not been decided, and, it seems to me, could not be decided without perversion of plain language, to apply to an arrangement by which competition is ended through community of interest—an arrangement which leaves the parties without external restriction.... But the act of Congress will not be construed to mean the universal disintegration of society into single men, each at war with all the rest, or even the prevention of all further combinations for a common end....

There is much that was mentioned in argument which I pass by. But in view of the great importance attached by both sides to the supposed attempt to suppress competition, I must say a word more about that. I said at the outset that I should assume, and I do assume, that one purpose of the purchase was to suppress competition between the two roads. I appreciate the force of the argument that there are independent stockholders in each; that it cannot be presumed that the respective boards of directors will propose any illegal act; that if they should they could be restrained, and that all that has been done as yet is too remote from the illegal result to be classed even as an attempt. Not every act done in furtherance of an unlawful end is an attempt or contrary to the law. There must be a certain nearness to the result. It is a question of proximity and degree. *Commonwealth v. Peasles,* 17 Massachusetts, 267, 272. So, as I have said, is the amenability of acts in furtherance of interference with commerce among the States to legislation by Congress. So, according to the intimation of this court, is the question of liability under the present statute. *Hopkins v. United States,* 171 U.S. 604. But I assume further, for the purposes of discussion, that what has been done is near enough to the result to fall under the law, if the law prohibits that result, although that assumption very nearly if not quite contradicts the decision in *United States v. E.C. Knight Co.,* 156 U.S. 1. But I say that the law does not prohibit the result. If it does it must be because there is some further meaning than I have yet discovered in the words "combinations in restraint of trade." I think that I have exhausted the meaning of those words in what I already have said. But they certainly do not require all existing competitions to be kept on foot, and, on the principle of the Trans-Missouri Freight Association's case, invalidate the continuance of old contracts by which former competitors united in the past....

To suppress competition in that way is one thing, to suppress it by fusion is another. The law, I repeat, says nothing about competition, and only prevents its suppression by contracts or combinations in restraint of trade, and such contracts or combinations derive their character as restraining trade from other features than the suppression of competition alone.... For, again I repeat, if the restraint on the freedom of the members of a combination caused by their entering into partnership is a restraint of trade, every such combination, as well as the small as the great, is within the act.

QUESTIONS

1. What does Justice Holmes mean by his statement that "great cases like hard cases make bad law"?
2. What, according to Holmes, is the real issue involved in this case? What mistakes does he believe the majority have made in holding the Northern Securities Company to be within the scope of the Sherman Act?

*Standard Oil Co. v. United States**

JUSTICE HARLAN, CONCURRING AND DISSENTING

... But, my brethren, in their wisdom,... have now said to those who condemn our former decisions and who object to all legislative prohibitions of contracts, combinations and trusts in restraint of interstate commerce, "You may now restrain such commerce, provided you are reasonable about it; only take care that the restraint is not undue." The disposition of the case under consideration, according to the views of the defendants, will, it is claimed quiet and give rest to "the business of the country." On the contrary, I have a strong conviction that it will throw the business of the country into confusion and invite widely-extended and harassing litigation, the injurious effects of which will be felt for many years to come. When Congress prohibited every contract, combination or monopoly, in restraint of commerce, it prescribed a simple, definite rule that all could understand, and which

*221 U.S. 1, 102–104, 105–106 (1911).

could be easily applied by everyone wishing to obey the law, and not to conduct their business in violation of law. But now, it is to be feared, we are to have, in cases without number, the constantly recurring inquiry—difficult to solve by proof—whether the particular contract, combination, or trust involved in each case is or is not an "unreasonable" or "undue" restraint of trade. Congress, in effect, said that there should be no restraint of trade, in any form, and this court solemnly adjudged many years ago that Congress meant what it thus said in clear and explicit words, and that it could not add to the words of the act. But those who condemn the action of Congress are now, in effect, informed that the courts will allow such restraints of interstate commerce as are shown not to be unreasonable or undue.

It remains for me to refer, more fully than I have heretofore done, to another, and, in my judgment—if we look to the future—the most important aspect of this case. That aspect concerns the usurpation by the judicial branch of the Government of the functions of the legislative department. The illustrious men who laid the foundations of our institutions, deemed no part of the National Constitution of more consequence or more essential to the permanency of our form of government than the provisions under which were distributed the powers of Government among three separate, equal and coordinate departments—legislative, executive, and judicial. This was at that time a new feature of governmental regulation among the nations of the earth, and it is deemed by the people of every section of our own country as most vital in the workings of a representative republic whose Constitution was ordained and established in order to accomplish the objects stated in its Preamble by the means, but only the means, provided either expressly or by necessary implication, by the instrument itself. No department of that government can constitutionally exercise the powers committed strictly to another and separate department. . . .

After many years of public service at the national Capital, and after a somewhat close observation of the conduct of public affairs, I am impelled to say that there is abroad, in our land, a most harmful tendency to bring about the amending of constitutions and legislative enactments by means alone of judicial construction. As a public policy has been declared by the legislative department in respect of interstate commerce, over which Congress has entire control, under the Constitution, all concerned must patiently submit to what has been lawfully done, until the People of the United States—the source of all National power—shall, in their own time, upon reflection and through the legislative department of the Government, require a change of that policy. There are some who say that it is a part of one's liberty to conduct commerce among the States without being subject to governmental authority. But that would not be liberty, regulated by law, and liberty, which cannot be regulated by law, is not to be desired. The Supreme Law of the Land—which is binding alike upon all—upon Presidents, Congresses, the Courts and the People—gives to Congress, and to Congress alone, authority to regulate interstate commerce, and when Congress forbids any restraint of such commerce, in any form, all must obey its mandate. To overreach the action of Congress merely by judicial construction, that is, by indirection, is a blow at the integrity of our governmental system, and in the end will prove most dangerous to all. Mr. Justice Bradley wisely said, when on this Bench, that illegitimate and unconstitutional practices get their first footing by silent approaches and slight deviations from legal modes of legal procedure. *Boyd v. United States,* 116 U.S. 616, 635. We shall do well to heed the warning of that great jurist. . . .

QUESTIONS

1.   Considering that Justice Harlan joined the Court in holding the Sherman Act applicable to Standard Oil, why is he so disturbed about the "rule of reason"?

2.   Is he correct in claiming that use of such a rule by the Court amounts to "usurpation by the judicial branch of the Government of the functions of the legislative department"?

VII.
Legal Education and the Legal Profession
1870–1900

Harvard Law School Entrance
Examinations *

1875 REQUIREMENTS

1. In Latin, in which subject candidates will be required to translate (without the aid of grammar or dictionary) passages selected from one or more of the following books: Caesar's Commentaries; Cicero's Orations and the Aeneid of Virgil.

2. In Blackstone's *Commentaries* (exclusive of Editor's notes).

3. Proficiency in French representing an amount of preparatory work equivalent to that demanded of those who offer Latin will be accepted as a substitute for the requisition of the latter language. Candidates will be required to translate (without the aid of grammar and dictionary) passages from standard French prose authors, and also to render into French, passages of easy English prose.

The Faculty will in their discretion permit some other language to be substituted for Latin or French, but a satisfactory examination in some language other than English will be insisted upon in all cases.

1878 ENTRANCE EXAMINATION EXCERPT

Translate:

Sacra Dioaeae matri divisque ferebam
Auspicibus coeptorum operum, superoque nitentem
Caelicolum regi mactabam in litore taurum.
Forte fuit iuxta tumulus, quo cornea summo
Virgulta et densis hastilibus horrida myrtus.
Accessi, viridemque ab humo convellere silvam
Conatus, ramis tegerem ut frondentibus aras,
Horrendum et dictu video mirabile monstrum.

---

* All excerpts from entrance examinations taken from Arthur E. Sutherland, *The Law at Harvard* (1967), pp. 168–169.

Nam, quae prima solo ruptis radicibus arbos
Vellitur, huic atro liquuntur sanguine guttae
Et terram tabo maculant.

1900 ENTRANCE EXAMINATION QUESTIONS BASED ON BLACKSTONE'S *COMMENTARIES*

1. What were the different kinds of guardian at common law? What were the duties of each?

2. What are the principal powers of a corporation? How may a corporation be dissolved?

3. What were the principal incidents of an estate tail?

4. A, owner of land in fee simple, wishes to give the following estates: to B for ten years, followed by an estate to C for C's life, followed by an estate to the eldest son of D, D being at the time a bachelor. How can A create these interests? What interest will each person have?

Suppose D does not marry until a year after the termination of the interest of B and C; what is the result?

5. What is an executory devise? Give examples.

6. Give two examples of redress of private wrong by mere act of the parties. What other remedy would have been available in either case?

7. What is a writ "de homine replegiando"? When is it used?

8. What was wager of law?

9. Name and explain three offenses against public trade.

10. What was the law as to arrest of offenders by a private individual?

*Charles W. Eliot, Harvard University President, Report, 1870–1871**

... A Law School which tries to do thorough work in this country has to contend with two traditions which still have an extraordinary force. The notion prevails that the way to learn Law is to go into a lawyer's office, see the outside of his business, copy papers for him, and read his books in the intervals of other employments. ... In this country the more successful a lawyer is the less he is inclined to spend time and thought in training inexperienced students; to teach is not considered a part of his professional business. The mere beginner can get little help from the lawyer into whose office he goes, unless the lawyer is a young man or an

---

* Harvard University, *Report of the President, 1870–1871.*

unsuccessful man who has abundant leisure, and even then the chances are that the amateur teacher will be inferior to the professional teachers in a Law School. A busy lawyer cannot be of much service to a student unless the student is capable of serving him. When a young man has thoroughly mastered at a good School the principles and methods of the Law,—when he has become familiar with Law books and has learned how to investigate and prepare a case, how to find precedents and how to use them,—he is ready to be of some service in a lawyer's office; he can do work of a higher grade than that of a copyist, and the more he can be trusted to go alone the more serviceable he will be, the more he will profit by his experience as a subordinate, and the shorter that experience will be. A young man should go into a lawyer's office after, and not before, he has been through a Law School, and even then not in the attitude of a student, but as an assistant or junior partner.

The second tradition with which Law Schools have to contend finds expression in the phrase "Reading Law." The idea conveyed by this phrase is that Law is to be learned by reading treatises and reports, the implication being that guidance and systematic instruction are superfluous. Now it would be hard to mention any subject in which the precept and example of a good teacher and thorough scholar can be of so much service to the student as in Law. Law is emphatically a science, with a method and a history; it has a language of its own, and a voluminous literature. The student needs direction as to the order of his studies; he needs, from day to day, guidance in selecting the raw material on which to expend his labor; he needs to be supplied with general criteria for discriminating between truth and error, between things essential and things adventitious; he needs to be shown how to disentangle principles from masses of encumbering detail; he needs to have the legal mode of thinking and reasoning exemplified for him, and to be exercised in it himself; he needs to be trained to seize and insist upon the material points of a case, and to use brevity, pertinency, and consecutiveness in speech. The positive instruction to be received from a superior mind well versed in the whole matter is of as much value to the student of Law as of any other science or liberal art. Moreover, the student requires to be personally drilled by reciting, writing opinions, drawing pleadings, and arguing cases. "Reading Law" is therefore an absurdly inadequate description of legal study....

QUESTIONS

1.   If an individual by "reading law," or by some other kind of preparation, can pass a state bar examination *without* regular attendance at or graduation from a law school, should he or she be permitted to practice law?

2.   How would Eliot respond to this question?

3.   On the basis of the knowledge you have acquired from your college courses thus far, could you answer correctly the questions posed in the admission tests to Harvard Law School as excerpted above?

The Diary of George T. Strong ‎

George T. Strong was a New York City resident and lawyer, with active interests in church, music, philanthropy and legal education as well as practice. He kept a diary for more than twenty-five years and, as is obvious from these excerpts, was a man of strong opinions.

APRIL 9, 1868

Bench and bar settle deeper in the mud every year and every month. They must be near the bottom now. Witness the indecencies...as reported in the newspapers....The Supreme Court is our *Cloaca Maxima* [deepest sewer], with lawyers for its rats.† But my simile does that rodent injustice, for the rat is a remarkably clean animal. (p. 202)

DECEMBER 19, 1868

Thus do we sink, bench and bar together. Any reaction must come soon, or we shall reach a stage of social gangrene and putrescence past help....The body politic of this city and country, judges, aldermen, councilmen, supervisors, and so on, our whole local government, is so diseased and so corrupt and so far gone that we can no longer count on any recuperative, restorative action of its vital forces....To be a citizen of New York is a disgrace. A domicile on Manhattan Island is a thing to be confessed with apologies and humiliation. The New Yorker belongs to a community worse governed by lower and baser blackguard scum

---

* *The Diary of George T. Strong,* ed. Allan Nevins and Milton Thomas (New York: Macmillan, 1951), vol. 4. Reprinted with permission of Macmillan Publishing Co., Inc. Copyright 1952 by Macmillan Publishing Co., Inc., renewed 1980 by Milton Halsey Thomas.

† Strong is referring here to the New York Supreme Court, a statewide trial court and not the highest court in New York, which is the Court of Appeals.

than any city in Western Christendom, or in the world, so far as I know. (p. 236)

MAY 20, 1869

[Commenting on speeches delivered at a Columbia Law School Commencement] It is notable that these four speeches... should each have been mainly an expression of the same thought... that corruption in our legislative bodies, our great corporations, and now even in the state judiciary... has at last reached a stage that must produce revolutionary action if no legal remedy can be found.... I verily believe we are nearly ripe for a Vigilance Committee.... The dishonesty of every man in public office is a violent presumption, and universally recognized as such. No decent man can take public office without imminent danger of losing caste, unless he can compel the respect of a defrauded but corrupt community by the accumulation of at least one or two millions of fraudulent profit. This state of things cannot last much longer without an explosion. (pp. 245-246)

OCTOBER 9, 1869

Application from three infatuated young women for admission to Law School. No woman shall degrade herself by practicing law, in New York especially, if I can save her.... "Women's-Rights Women" are uncommonly loud and offensive of late. I loathe the lot. The first effect of their success would be the introduction into society of a third sex, without the grace of woman or the vigor of man; and then woman, being physically the weaker vessel and having thrown away the protection of her present honors and immunities, would become what the squaw is to the male of her species—a drudge and domestic animal.... (p. 256)

DECEMBER 18, 1869

The stink of our state judiciary is growing too strongly ammoniac and hippuric [smelly] for endurance.... We "do smell all h———p———" whenever we read or hear about the sayings or doings of the average New York judge. He is as bad as the New York alderman, if not worse, because his office is more sacred. People begin to tire of holding their noses, and are looking about in a helpless way for some remedy. The nuisance must be abated somehow... but I see no hope... except by a most perilous process, justified only by the extremest necessity, and after all constitutional remedies are exhausted.... Law protects life no longer.... The abused machinery of Law is a terror to property owners.... A judge of our Supreme Court is *prima facie* disreputable.... I verily believe that by pulling one or two strings, I could obtain "an allowance" of $150,000... but the joke would be indecent—a profane trifling over the corpse of a profession that was once most honored and noble. (pp. 264-265)

DECEMBER 21, 1869

I think Nature meant Cardozo* to sweep the court room, not to preside in it, and that he would look more natural in the dock of the Sessions than on the Bench of the Supreme Court. (p. 265)

JANUARY 25, 1870

Crime was never so bold, so frequent, and so safe as it is this winter. We breathe an atmosphere of highway robbery, burglary, and murder. Few criminals are caught, and fewer punished. Municipal law is a failure in New York, and we must soon fall back on the law of self preservation. (p. 271)

APRIL 17, 1870

[Commenting on the proposed nomination of "one Spencer, a Justice of the Superior Court" to be a member of the Trinity Church governing board] When his name was brought up... His position on the bench was held a fatal objection to him. He must have been put there with the approval of the Ring† and is, therefore, open to violent suspicion of being everything a vestryman of Trinity Church should not be. The objection is unanswerable, but what an illustration it is of the degradation of this city! A seat on the bench of the Superior Court... is now *prima facie* evidence of dishonesty.... (p. 283)

APRIL 21, 1871

The state legislature is about to become inodorous and adjourn.... Boss Tweed and his tail are sovereigns of this city and county. Perhaps the title "Boss of New York" will grow into permanence and

---

* The Cardozo mentioned by Strong was the father of Benjamin Cardozo, later to become one of the most distinguished justices—both of the New York Court of Appeals, and of the United States Supreme Court, where he succeeded Justice Holmes.
† The term "Ring" was the popular title for the Tweed machine; thus the word was, for Strong at least, synonymous with graft and corruption.

figure in history like that of the doge of Venice. All titles have their beginnings, and we may be ruled henceforth by a series of bosses, hereditary or nominally elective. (p. 352)

JULY 22, 1871

The [New York] Times is creating a deep sensation by detailed statements of vast sums embezzled by the Ring, with names, dates, and amounts. Some clerk in the Comptroller's office has been bought, no doubt. An unclean job, but one must fight the Devil with fire. (p. 375)

JULY 26, 1871

But the minds of a New York assemblage are as running water. The impressions of today are effaced tomorrow. The disease of this community lies too deep to be cured by meetings, resolutions, and committees. We the people are a low set, without moral virility. Our rulers, Tweed and Company, are about good enough for us. (p. 382)

SEPTEMBER 6, 1871

[Refers to Mr. Justice Barnard, an official linked to the Ring] By appearing in the new role of an honest and fearless judge he may escape mischief and gain much *kudos* [praise] with unthinking people. These considerations may lead him sorrowfully to decline the huge bribe that is doubtless within his reach and try to act with the semblance of uprightness.... But he is an evil beast and will probably aim at amusing the reformers, without doing substantial harm to his old allies in corruption. (pp. 382–383)

SEPTEMBER 22, 1871

But I fear our labor for reform will be in vain. We may succeed in breaking this Ring, but another will soon be riveted around our necks. A sordid and depraved community cannot govern itself without corruption. Cutting out a cancer or a gangrenous spot does not *cure* a patient whose blood is thoroughly poisoned.... When we the people learn ... to consider wealth basely acquired and ignobly enjoyed a reproach and not a glory, we shall have a right to hope for honest rulers. (p. 386)

OCTOBER 25, 1871

Reform organizations are wide-awake and make good nominations.... Tweed's impudent serenity is sublime. Were he not a supreme scoundrel, he would be a great man. (p. 394)

OCTOBER 28, 1871

Tweed magnanimously submitted to arrest yesterday, and was held on bail for one million dollars.... Tweed is a grand moral spectacle— statuesque as a demigod in Greek tragedy. (p. 395)

DECEMBER 16, 1871

The Bar Association is pusillanimous; its members are afraid to get up a case against Barnard, Cardozo and Company, though abundant proof of corruption is within their reach. If they should fail, Barnard and the others would be hostile to them, and they would lose clients.... I feel inclined to resign from this Bar Association. (p. 404)

FEBRUARY 3, 1872

We are living in a day of ruffianism and of almost universal corruption. Life and property are as insecure here in New York as in Mexico. It is a thoroughly rotten community.... Unless some peaceful and lawful remedy is found, a dangerous convulsion cannot be far off. To degrade venal judges and restore confidence in the courts is manifestly the first step towards reform.... (p. 411)

MARCH 25, 1872

I fear our trouble lies deeper than the venality of legislature and judiciary. I fear the community has lost all moral sense and moral tone, and is fast becoming too rotten to live. We are seriously threatened by social disintegration and a general smash. I wish I could flee into the wilderness... and take refuge in some dull but decent New England village. (p. 419)

MAY 31, 1873

[The Albany legislature] has disbanded at last, to the great relief of all honest men. Such a crew of buccaneers has seldom been got together since the days of Captain Kidd. They were nearly all "on the make." (p. 482)

DECEMBER 26, 1873

[Commenting on the acquittal of one member of the Ring] That he got none of the money is likely enough. His corrupt inducement may have been merely the implied promise of political promotion. . . . But he has come very near joining his politic ally Tweed, the vanished King Arthur of their shattered Ring, for whom civic scoundrelism weeps and wails and looks out in vain. (p. 507)

QUESTIONS

1. How do these excerpts reflect the changes in the urban bar discussed at the end of Chapter 3?

2. Note Strong's comments on July 22, 1871, concerning the "expose" in the *New York Times* of the Tweed Ring's activities. Strong observes that "some clerk in the Comptroller's Office has been bought, no doubt. An unclean job, but one must fight the Devil with fire." What does he mean? What relevance does his statement have for ethics and the practice of law?

Bibliographic Essay

This essay makes no pretense at providing extensive coverage for further reading in American legal history between 1865 and 1915. It does, however, suggest additional sources for the topics discussed in this book.

The best general overview of this period of American history may well be Robert Wiebe, *The Search for Order* (1967). Rich in insights if not in specifics, the book examines the growing complexity of American society after the Civil War. There is no comparable overview for American legal history, although Lawrence Friedman devotes a good deal of space to it in *A History of American Law* (1973). Because of its very complex character, a comprehensive overview of American legal history remains a dream, not a reality. For my comments on some of the problems inherent in Friedman's work see book review by Jonathan Lurie in *Rutgers Law Review,* 27 (1974), 354–363. Willard Hurst has written extensively on American legal history; *Law and the Conditions of Freedom in Nineteenth-Century United States* (1956) remains his most readable work. Hurst has undertaken a somewhat generalized analysis in "Legal Elements in United States History," *Perspectives in American History,* 5 (1971). Morton Keller has provided an impressive synthesis of domestic political development in *Affairs of State* (1977). Grant Gilmore, *Ages of American Law* (1977), a short book of lectures, is strongly recommended; written by a distinguished but totally unpretentious legal scholar, the result is a short overview of American legal history that is stimulating and informative but in no way pedantic. Two case studies that have methodological significance for understanding law and public policy during the late nineteenth century are Lee Benson, *Merchants, Farmers and Railroads: Railroad Regulation and New York Politics, 1850–1877* (1955), and George Miller, *Railroads and the Granger Laws* (1971). Several anthologies of articles dealing with American legal history have been published within the last ten years. The best of these is Lawrence Friedman and Harry Scheiber (eds.),

171

American Law and the Constitutional Order (1978). See also Wythe Holt (ed.), *Essays in Nineteenth-Century American Legal History* (1976).

For a comprehensive legal history of the Reconstruction era, see the last six chapters of Harold Hyman and William Wiecek, *Equal Justice Under Law* (1982). Although this work stands as a major contribution to the field, I believe that the authors place too much emphasis on the "intentional" linkage between the Thirteenth Amendment, the Civil Rights Act of 1866, and the Fourteenth Amendment. On the other hand, Hyman and Wiecek do a superb job of showing the incredibly complex patterns of changing theories and beliefs concerning federalism, civil rights, Reconstruction, and the law, between 1865 and 1875. They also include a useful and thorough bibliography.

The controversy over what the framers intended concerning the Fourteenth Amendment continues, generating much heat but little else. While written for a different purpose than presenting the historical origins of the amendment, two articles that include adequate historical treatment are Charles Fairman, "Does the Fourteenth Amendment Incorporate the Bill of Rights?" *Stanford Law Review*, 2 (1949), 5-139, an exhaustive and exhausting article (more than 100 pages and almost 400 citations); and Alexander M. Bickel, "The Original Understanding," *Harvard Law Review*, 69 (1955), 1-65, a more satisfactory analysis. Fairman argues that the framers did not intend that the Bill of Rights be made applicable to the states by the new amendment. Bickel concludes that the framers knew they were dealing with an amendment to American organic law, that they deliberately used broad language in the amendment, and that they fully expected future courts and judges to interpret its scope and meaning. Raoul Berger, *Government by Judiciary* (1977), concludes that the Supreme Court has consistently if not continually distorted the intentions of the framers concerning the Fourteenth Amendment; this is a work that remains interesting if at the same time unconvincing. The general development of the Fourteenth Amendment since 1868 is traced in a series of excellent though difficult essays by Howard Jay Graham, *Everyman's Constitution* (1968). The adoption of the Fourteenth Amendment and the initial reaction of the United States Supreme Court to it is discussed in Charles Fairman, *Reconstruction and Reunion, 1864-1888* (1971). Poorly organized and poorly edited, sprawling over a multiplicity of unnecessary details, Fairman's book is a disappointing volume in a multivolume history of the United States Supreme Court—the Oliver Wendell Holmes Devise—that sadly has turned out to be less than distinguished, at least thus far. Herman Belz, *Emancipation and Civil Rights* (1978), presents a readable synthesis, although I do not agree with Belz's contention that the term "civil rights" means more today than it did in the 1860s. See also David Donald, *Charles Sumner and the Rights of Man* (1970), the second volume in Donald's biography of Sumner. The reasons why the Civil War generation was ill prepared to move toward genuine racial reforms are convincingly analyzed by Phillip Paludan in *A Covenant with Death* (1975). William Gillette, *Retreat from Reconstruction* (1979), is an excellent synthesis of this period. Although dealing with the 1954 case of *Brown v. Board of Education,* Richard Kluger, *Simple Justice* (1975), has a wealth of background on early civil rights cases from 1868 on; this is an impressive history.

A good source for an introduction to the growth of corporate enterprise in this period is Glenn Porter, *The Rise of Big Business, 1860–1910* (1973). Several chapters in Willard Hurst's study *Growth of American Law: The Law Makers* (1950) provide good introductory background. See also Hurst's more recent series of lectures, *The Legitimacy of the Business Corporation in the Law of the United States, 1780–1970* (1970). Two studies that adequately analyze the role of lawyers and judges toward the legal conservatism of the late nineteenth century are Benjamin Twiss, *Lawyers and the Constitution* (1942), and Clyde Jacobs, *Law Writers and the Courts* (1954). Both are inferior, however, to Arnold Paul, *Conservative Crisis and the Rule of Law: Attitudes of Bar and Bench, 1887–1895* (1960). Paul attempts to show the broader social values that influenced both courts and lawyers. A good, as well as sympathetic, biography of Chief Justice Morrison R. Waite, who handed down the decision in *Munn v. Illinois,* is C. Peter Magrath, *Morrison R. Waite—The Triumph of Character* (1963). See also an earlier study of the spokesman for the Court in *Slaughter-House:* Charles Fairman, *Mr. Justice Miller and the Supreme Court 1862–1890* (1930).

Scholars are just beginning to explore in some detail the evolution of American administrative law. Some of the very vague contours are noted briefly in Harold Hyman, *A More Perfect Union* (1973), an excellent study. See also, Thomas K. McCraw, "Regulation in America: A Review Article," *Business History Review* 49 (1975), 150–183. One attempt to analyze the evolution of a private mercantile club into an important private regulatory agency is Jonathan Lurie, *The Chicago Board of Trade, 1859–1905: The Dynamics of Self-Regulation* (1979). Alfred Chandler, Jr., *The Visible Hand: The Managerial Revolution in American Business* (1977), discusses the interaction between industrial, managerial, and administrative regulation. See also the relevant sections in Morton Keller, *Affairs of State* (1977).

Much of the vast literature about regulatory commissions centers on their alleged ineffectiveness in dealing with the very forces they are supposed to regulate. Some historical analysis of the origins of the regulatory commission may be found in Frank Hendrick, *Railroad Control by Commissions* (1900). See also the first systematic study of an American regulatory commission: I.L. Sharfman, *The Interstate Commerce Commission* (1931–1937), a bulky, ponderous study but one that still has great value. A much shorter and more critical history of the I.C.C. is by Ari Hoogenboom and Olive Hoogenboom, *A History of the I.C.C.—From Panacea to Palliative* (1976).

The origins of the Sherman Act are detailed in Hans Thorelli, *The Federal Antitrust Policy* (1955). See also William Letwin, *Law and Economic Policy in America* (1965). There is a wealth of contemporary comment on concentration and monopoly in numerous volumes of the *North American Review*, the *Nation*, and *Atlantic Monthly*, to mention only a few. See in particular the years 1888–1890. Other extremely important sources, especially for legal history, are some of the law journals published during the late nineteenth century, such as the *American Law Review*, the *Albany Law Journal*, and the *American Law Register*.

Any study of the American legal profession should begin with Alfred Z. Reed, *Training for the Public Profession of the Law* (1921). Robert Stevens has updated many of Reed's conclusions, in "Two Cheers for 1870: The American Law School," *Perspectives in American History*, 5 (1971). Two studies of Harvard Law School should be noted: Arthur Sutherland, *The Law at Harvard: A History of Ideas and Men, 1817–1967* (1967), an affectionate and for the most part uncritical account by a distinguished professor at the school; and Joel Seligman, *The High Citadel: The Influence of Harvard Law School* (1978). The latter work, although written, according to Seligman, with a sense of affection for Harvard Law School, from which he graduated, is very critical of the institution. It also has an introduction by Ralph Nader, to whom the book is dedicated, and Nader refers to Harvard Law School as "a stagnating phenomenon still clothed with ermine." Mention should also be made of Jerold Auerbach, *Unequal Justice: Lawyers and Social Change in Modern America* (1976). Auerbach claims that the organized American legal profession has tended to value process rather than substance and has paid scant attention to its social responsibility. The result is a profession with elitist overtones that tends, he argues, to subvert the very equality of justice to which the American bar is supposedly dedicated. For a very interesting reaction to the book from a member of this elite, see the review by federal judge Charles E. Wyzanski, Jr., in *Harvard Law Review*, 90 (1976), 283–290.

An able assessment of the legal profession in transition is Maxwell Bloomfield, *American Lawyers in a Changing Society 1776–1876* (1976). For an independent history of the Bar Association of New York, see George Martin, *Causes and Conflicts* (1970). As Martin notes (p. 39), the *Diary of George Templeton Strong* (1952) is a very important source—not just for the changing perceptions of and by the legal profession but for American life in general during the late nineteenth century. On the establishment of the American Bar Association, see the appropriate articles in *American Bar Association Journal*, 64 (1978). The transformation of American legal education must be seen against the backdrop of the transformation of the American university in general during the late nineteenth century. An outstanding study of this subject is Laurence Veysey, *The Emergence of the American University* (1965).

The career of Theodore Roosevelt has spawned a vast number of books, but there has been very little relating his actions and ideas to the legal order and the role of lawyers. The place to begin is the last three volumes of Roosevelt's indispensable *Letters*, edited by Elting Morison (1954). The best study of TR prior to his assumption of the presidency is Edmund Morris, *The Rise of Theodore Roosevelt* (1979). Although the final volume in that study has yet to be published, Morris presents a superb preview of it in "Theodore Roosevelt, President," *American Heritage*, 32 (1981). For information on Simeon Baldwin, especially the Baldwin-Roosevelt battle over workmen's compensation, see Charles C. Goetsch, *Essays on Simeon E. Baldwin* (1981). In addition to the sources cited there, see also Carl Auerbach, Willard Hurst, Lloyd Garrison, and Samuel Mermin, *The Legal Process* (1961). Three articles that discuss the development of an American response to industrial accidents are Lawrence M. Friedman and Jack Ladinsky, "Social Change and the Law of Industrial Accidents," *Columbia Law Review*, 67 (1967), 50–82; Lawrence Friedman, "Legal Rules and the Process of Social Change," *Stanford Law Review*, 19 (1967), 786–840; and Jonathan Lurie, "Lawyers, Judges , and Legal Change, 1852–1916: New York as a Case Study," *Working Papers, Regional Economic History Research Center*, 3 (1980), 31–56. Insights are also found in Roosevelt's *Autobiography* (1913). The short study by John M. Blum, *The Republican Roosevelt* (1954), remains extremely valuable. William Harbaugh's biography of Roosevelt, *The Life and Times of Theodore Roosevelt: Power and Responsibility* (1975), is strongly recommended and also has a very good bibliographic essay.

About the Author

JONATHAN LURIE received his B.A. and M.A.T. from Harvard University. He was awarded the Ph.D. from the University of Wisconsin in 1970. At Rutgers University, Newark, since 1969, Professor Lurie has served as Associate Dean and Acting Dean of the Graduate School-Rutgers, Newark, and is currently chairman and associate professor of the history department, specializing in American legal history, as well as an adjunct associate professor at Rutgers Law School. A recipient of fellowships from the American Bar Foundation, the Russell Sage Foundation, and the Social Sciences Research Council, in 1973-1974 he was a Visiting Liberal Arts Fellow at Harvard Law School, and in 1978-1979 he received an N.E.H. research grant for study of American state courts and civil liberties during the late nineteenth century, the subject of a forthcoming book. His first book, *The Chicago Board of Trade, 1859-1905,* was published in 1979.

A Note on the Type

The text of this book was set in a computer version of Times Roman, designed by Stanley Morison for *The Times* (London) and first introduced by that newspaper in 1932.

Among typographers and designers of the twentieth century, Stanley Morison has been a strong forming influence as typographical adviser to the English Monotype Corporation, as a director of two distinguished English publishing houses, and as a writer of sensibility, erudition, and keen practical sense.

Typography by Barbara Sturman. Cover design by Maria Epes. Composition by Delmas Typesetting, Ann Arbor, Michigan. Printed and bound by Banta Company, Menasha, Wisconsin.

Index

BORZOI BOOKS
IN LAW AND AMERICAN SOCIETY

Law and American History

EARLY AMERICAN LAW AND SOCIETY
Stephen Botein, *Michigan State University*

This volume consists of an essay dealing with the nature of law and early American socioeconomic development from the first settlements to 1776. The author shows how many legal traditions sprang both from English experience and from the influence of the New World. He explores the development of transatlantic legal structures in order to show how they helped rationalize intercolonial affairs. Mr. Botein also emphasizes the relationship between law and religion. The volume includes a pertinent group of documents for classroom discussion, and a bibliographic essay.

LAW IN THE NEW REPUBLIC: *Private Law and the Public Estate*
George Dargo, *Brookline, Massachusetts*

Though the American Revolution had an immediate and abiding impact on American public law (e.g., the formation of the federal and state constitutions), its effect on private law (e.g., the law of contracts, tort law) was less direct but of equal importance. Through essay and documents, Mr. Dargo examines post-Revolutionary public and private reform impulses and finds a shifting emphasis from public to private law which he terms "privatization." To further illustrate the tension between public and private law, the author develops a case study (the Batture land controversy in New Orleans) in early nineteenth century legal, economic, and political history. The volume includes a wide selection of documents and a bibliographic essay.

LAW IN ANTEBELLUM SOCIETY: *Legal Change and Economic Expansion*
Jamil Zainaldin, *Washington, D.C.*

This book examines legal change and economic expansion in the first half of the nineteenth century, integrating major themes in the development of law with key historical themes. Through a series of topical essays and the use of primary source materials, it describes how political, social, and economic interests and values influence law making. The book's focus is on legislation and the common law.

LAW AND THE NATION, 1865–1912
Jonathan Lurie, *Rutgers University*

Using the Fourteenth Amendment as the starting point for his essay, Mr. Lurie examines the ramifications of this landmark constitutional provision on the economic and social development of America in the years following the Civil War. He also explores important late nineteenth-century developments in legal education, and concludes his narrative with some insights on law and social change in the first decade of the twentieth century. The volume is highlighted by a documents section containing statutes, judicial opinions, and legal briefs, with appropriate questions for classroom discussion. Mr. Lurie's bibliographic essay provides information to stimulate further investigation of this period.

ORDERED LIBERTY: *Legal Reform in the Twentieth Century*
Gerald L. Fetner, *University of Chicago*

In an interpretive essay, the author examines the relationship between several major twentieth-century reform movements (e.g., Progressivism, New Deal, and the Great Society) and the law. He shows how policy makers turned increasingly to the legal community for assistance in accommodating economic and social conflict, and how the legal profession responded by formulating statutes, administrative agencies, and private arrangements. Mr. Fetner also discusses how the organization and character of the legal profession were affected by these social changes. Excerpts from relevant documents illustrate issues discussed in the essay. A bibliographic essay is included.

Law and Philosophy

DISCRIMINATION AND REVERSE DISCRIMINATION
R. Kent Greenawalt, *Columbia Law School*

Using discrimination and reverse discrimination as a model, Mr. Greenawalt examines the relationship between law and ethics. He finds that the proper role of law cannot be limited to grand theory concerning individual liberty and social restraint, but must address what law can effectively discover and accomplish. Such concepts as distributive and compensatory justice and utility are examined in the context of preferential treatment for blacks and other minorities. The analysis draws heavily on the Supreme Court's Bakke decision. The essay is followed by related documents, primarily judicial opinions, with notes and questions, and a bibliography.

THE LEGAL ENFORCEMENT OF MORALITY
Thomas Grey, *Stanford Law School*

This book deals with the traditional issue of whether morality can be legislated and enforced. It consists of an introductory essay and legal texts on three issues: the enforcement of sexual morality, the treatment of human remains, and the duties of potential rescuers. The author shows how philosophical problems differ from classroom hypotheticals when they are confronted in a legal setting. He illustrates this point using material from statutes, regulations, judicial opinions, and law review commentaries. Mr. Grey reviews the celebrated Hart-Devlin debate over the legitimacy of prohibiting homosexual acts. He places the challenging problem of how to treat dead bodies, arising out of developments in the technology of organ transplantation, in the context of the debate over morals enforcement, and discusses the Good Samaritan as an issue concerning the propriety of the legal enforcement of moral duties.

LEGAL REASONING
Martin Golding, *Duke University*

This volume is a blend of text and readings. The author explores the many sides to legal reasoning—as a study in judicial psychology and, in a more narrow sense, as an inquiry into the "logic" of judicial decision making. He shows how judges justify their rulings, and gives examples of the kinds of arguments they use. He challenges the notion that judicial reasoning is rationalization; instead, he argues that judges are guided by a deep concern for consistency and by a strong need to have their decisions stand as a measure for the future conduct of individuals. *(Forthcoming in 1984)*

Law and American Literature

LAW AND AMERICAN LITERATURE
A one-volume collection of the following three essays:

Law as Form and Theme in American Letters
Carl S. Smith, *Northwestern University*

The author explores the interrelationships between law aned literature generally and between American law and American literature in particular. He explores first the literary qualities of legal writing and then the attitudes of major American writers toward the law. Throughout, he studies the links between the legal and literary imaginations. He finds that legal writing has many literary qualities that are essential to its function, and he points out that American writers have long been wary of the power of the law and its special language, speaking out as a compensating voice for the ideal of justice.

Innocent Criminal or Criminal Innocence: The Trial in American Fiction
John McWilliams, *Middlebury College*

Mr. McWilliams explores how law functions as a standard for conduct in a number of major works of American literature, including Cooper's *The Pioneers,* Melville's *Billy Budd,* Dreiser's *An American Tragedy,* and Wright's *Native Son.* Each of these books ends in a criminal trial, in which the reader is asked to choose between his emotional sympathy for the victim and his rational understanding of society's need for criminal sanctions. The author compares these books with James Gould Cozzens' *The Just and the Unjust,* a study of a small town legal system, in which the people's sense of justice contravenes traditional authority.

Law and Lawyers in American Popular Culture
Maxwell Bloomfield, *Catholic University of America*

Melding law, literature, and the American historical experience into a single essay, Mr. Bloomfield discusses popular images of the lawyer. The author shows how contemporary values and attitudes toward the law are reflected in fiction. He concentrates on two historical periods: antebellum America and the Progressive era. He examines fictional works which were not always literary classics, but which exposed particular legal mores. An example of such a book is Winston Churchill's *A Far Country* (1915), a story of a successful corporation lawyer who abandons his practice to dedicate his life to what he believes are more socially desirable objectives.